HOW TO RESIST amazon AND WHY

UPDATED & EXPANDED

THE FIGHT FOR **Local Economies**, **Data Privacy**, **Fair Labor**, **Independent Bookstores**, AND A **People-Powered Future**

DANNY CAINE

Microcosm Publishing
Portland, Ore

HOW TO RESIST AMAZON AND WHY

THE FIGHT FOR **Local Economies, Data Privacy, Fair Labor, Independent Bookstores,** AND A **People-Powered Future**

© 2021-2022 Danny Caine
© This edition Microcosm Publishing 2021-2022
Second edition - 7,000 copies - September 20, 2022
Originally published 2021
ISBN 9781648411236
This is Microcosm #589
Cover by Matt Gauck and Joe Biel
Edited by Lydia Rogue

To join the ranks of high-class stores that feature Microcosm titles, talk to your local rep: In the U.S. **COMO** (Atlantic), **FUJII** (Midwest), **BOOK TRAVELERS WEST** (Pacific), **TURNAROUND** (Europe), **UTP/MANDA** (Canada), **NEW SOUTH** (Australia/New Zealand), **GPS** in Asia, Africa, India, South America, and other countries, or **FAIRE** in the gift trade.

For a catalog, write or visit:
Microcosm Publishing
2752 N Williams Ave.
Portland, OR 97227
https://microcosm.pub/htra

Did you know that you can buy our books directly from us at sliding scale rates? Support a small, independent publisher and pay less than Amazon's price at **www.Microcosm.Pub**

Library of Congress Cataloging-in-Publication Data

Names: Caine, Danny, author.
Title: How to resist Amazon and why : the fight for local economics, data privacy, fair labor, independent bookstores, and a people-powered future! / by Danny Caine.
Description: [Second edition] | [Portland] : Microcosm Publishing, [2022] | Includes bibliographical references. | Summary: "When a company's workers are literally dying on the job, when their business model relies on preying on local businesses and even their own vendors, when their CEO is the richest person in the world while their workers make low wages with impossible quotas... wouldn't you want to resist? Danny Caine, owner of Raven Book Store in Lawrence, Kansas has been an outspoken critic of the seemingly unstoppable Goliath of the bookselling world: Amazon. In this book, he lays out the case for shifting our personal money and civic investment away from global corporate behemoths and to small, local, independent businesses. Well-researched and lively, his tale covers the history of big box stores, the big political drama of delivery, and the perils of warehouse work. He shows how Amazon's ruthless discount strategies mean authors, publishers, and even Amazon themselves can lose money on every book sold. And he spells out a clear path to resistance, in a world where consumers are struggling to get by. In-depth research is interspersed with charming personal anecdotes from bookstore life, making this a readable, fascinating, essential book for the 2020s"-- Provided by publisher.
Identifiers: LCCN 2022014755 | ISBN 9781648411236 (trade paperback)
Subjects: LCSH: Amazon.com (Firm) | Bezos, Jeffrey. | Small business. | Independent bookstores. | Pay equity.
Classification: LCC HF5548.32 .C33 2022 | DDC 381/.142--dc23/eng/20220329
LC record available at https://lccn.loc.gov/2022014755

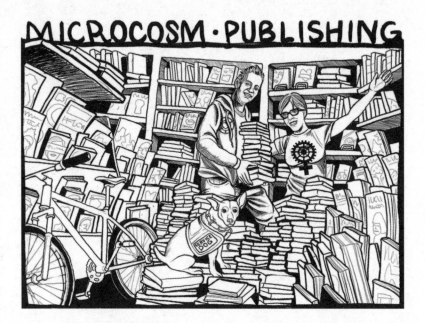

MICROCOSM PUBLISHING is Portland's most diversified publishing house and distributor with a focus on the colorful, authentic, and empowering. Our books and zines have put your power in your hands since 1996, equipping readers to make positive changes in their lives and in the world around them. Microcosm emphasizes skill-building, showing hidden histories, and fostering creativity through challenging conventional publishing wisdom with books and bookettes about DIY skills, food, bicycling, gender, self-care, and social justice. What was once a distro and record label was started by Joe Biel in his bedroom and has become among the oldest independent publishing houses in Portland, OR. We are a politically moderate, centrist publisher in a world that has inched to the right for the past 80 years.

Global labor conditions are bad, and our roots in industrial Cleveland in the 70s and 80s made us appreciate the need to treat workers right. Therefore, our books are MADE IN THE USA.

Dedicated to the workers.

CONTENTS

PREFACE TO THE 2ND EDITION 9

INTRODUCTION 13
WHY *HOW TO RESIST AMAZON AND WHY*

INTERLUDE ONE 21
A LETTER TO JEFF BEZOS FROM A SMALL BOOKSTORE IN THE MIDDLE
OF THE COUNTRY

CHAPTER ONE 25
ON AMAZON AND THE BOOK INDUSTRY

INTERLUDE TWO 41
ON SMALL BUSINESS AND POLITICS

CHAPTER TWO 47
ON AMAZON'S JOBS

INTERLUDE THREE 69
ON WHETHER AMAZON AFFECTS MY WORK AT THE RAVEN

CHAPTER THREE 73
ON AMAZON'S FULFILLMENT PIPELINE

INTERLUDE FOUR 85
ON RAVEN'S ALL-TIME BEST SELLER

CHAPTER FOUR 89
ON AMAZON'S RELATIONSHIP TO PRIVACY AND SURVEILLANCE

INTERLUDE FIVE 101
ON PARTNERING WITH AUTHORS

CHAPTER FIVE 105
ON AMAZON'S EVERYTHING STORE PROBLEM

INTERLUDE SIX 117
ON BORDERS

CHAPTER SIX 121
ON AMAZON AND THE ENVIRONMENT

INTERLUDE SEVEN 133
ON ART, ACTIVISM, AND AMAZON

CHAPTER SEVEN 139
ON AMAZON AND THE GOVERNMENT

INTERLUDE EIGHT 157
ON DELIGHTS

CHAPTER EIGHT 161
HOW TO RESIST AMAZON

CHAPTER NINE 175
CONCLUSION

APPENDIX 178
FOR FURTHER READING

ACKNOWLEDGEMENTS 182
SOURCES CITED

ABOUT THE AUTHOR 190

PREFACE TO THE 2ND EDITION

*T*n November, 2021, a tweet by @tanyaboza was making the rounds on Writing Twitter. The tweet read, "If you are working on a nonfiction book right now, can you state the core argument in one tweet?" Since I had just begun putting together the research for this second edition, I retweeted the prompt, summarizing this book's argument as, simply, "Amazon is bad."

Five minutes later, @AmazonHelp replied: "We're sorry for the experience. Without providing any account or personal details, can you give us more insight on the issue you've encountered? Let us know. We're here to help however we can. -Angela." Oh, Angela. Where do I even start?

I didn't know how Angela at @AmazonHelp found me, nor why she so badly misunderstood the context of my tweet. Nowhere in my Tweet had I tagged Amazon. Maybe "Angela" is some sort of bot that's trained to scan all of Twitter for phrases like "Amazon is bad." Who knows. What I did know: "Angela" was one of many, many examples telling me there was more work to be done with this little book.

I turned in the final draft for the first edition of *How to Resist Amazon and Why* in October, 2020. That means I didn't know who was going to win the 2020 presidential election. For that matter, I didn't know that seditious terrorists would raid the U.S. Capitol on January 6, 2021. I also didn't know that this tiny book would travel around the world, stocked in countless bookstores, starting countless conversations about big tech, monopolies, and small businesses. I didn't know a bookstore friend of mine would give a copy of it during her family's Amazon-themed secret santa. I didn't know it would be the #1 nonfiction bestseller of 2021 at Evanston, IL's Bookends and Beginnings. I didn't know the owner of Bookends and Beginnings, my friend Nina Barrett, would become deeply involved in a legal fight to curb Amazon's monopoly power.

So as you see, there was a lot I didn't know when I turned in the first version of *How to Resist Amazon and Why*. But a few specific things really motivated me to return to this book and revise it: that Amazon workers at the fulfillment center in Bessemer, Alabama would launch a historic union drive at their warehouse. That this effort, easily the largest yet in Amazon's history, would generate huge interest and discussion about Amazon's labor practices. That Amazon would engage in one of the most expensive, elaborate, and ruthless union busting campaigns in history to ultimately squash the union's efforts. That the National Labor Relations Board would deem Amazon's actions so inappropriate that they'd mandate a re-vote. That the Bessemer union drive was a major early moment in a massive, nationwide labor movement that included mass resignations, increased union activity, and renewed fervor in the discussion of workers' rights. That this labor movement would touch every industry, including my own.

When I finished the first draft of *How to Resist Amazon and Why*, I did not know that a tornado would hit an Amazon warehouse in Edwardsville, Illinois. I did not know that Amazon's negligence, from keeping workers on their routes in severe weather to banning phones on warehouse floors, might have led to the warehouse's six deaths.

On top of that, I did not know that Amazon allowed Chinese authorities to censor all but 5-star reviews of Xi Jinping's book. I did not know that Amazon had started a high school program to spread pro-Amazon propaganda to students. I did not know that Jeff Bezos had commissioned a boat so big, a historic bridge would have to be removed in order for it to leave the shipyard. I did not know that upon returning from his first Blue Origin spaceflight, Bezos would say the quiet part loud by saying Amazon workers "paid for all this." I did not know that both the boat and the spaceflight quip would be used by union organizers to drum up support for a historic and unprecedented union drive in Staten Island. I did not know the full extent to which Amazon's dominance (and spaceflight hobby) adversely impacted our planet's climate.

But this book was never meant to be all doom-and-gloom. I wanted to celebrate resistance as much as I wanted to decry Amazon's crimes. So I wanted to return to it so I could tell you about the poet who spent years quietly reviewing Amazon products with gorgeous and lyrical personal essays. About the artists gaming and pranking Amazon's algorithms to intriguing effect. About France successfully outlawing loss-leading shipping on books, a meaningful gesture at bolstering its bookstore community. About the House Judiciary Committee's monumental big tech investigation turning into a historic package of 5 bills, whose bipartisan support might actually lead to government action to break up big tech monopolies. About antitrust superstar Lina Khan not only being named to the FTC, but being selected as its chair, joining other antimonopoly crusaders like Tim Wu and Jonathan Kanter in highly influential government positions.

When I turned in the first edition of *How to Resist Amazon and Why*, I did not know I'd get a chance to write a second edition. I'm so glad the folks at Microcosm decided to give it a go. Revisiting this book will give me a chance to correct, add to, and improve the original, bringing it up to date and giving proper due to the above-mentioned topics and more. I haven't just added a few new chunks of text; I've gone through line by line, expanding and adding to all the original chapters, in the process doubling the number of citations from work by amazing writers and dogged reporters. In addition, I've added a new chapter about Amazon and the climate, plus a new interlude about the artists who are working within and around Amazon to raise these issues via art. All told, 40% of the book you hold is new material.

While I'm thankful for the chance to update and revise this book to include important developments like the Bessemer union drive and the House Judiciary's 5 big tech bills, the idea of having a perfectly up-to-date book is an impossible dream, especially for a print book. The earliest you'll hold this book is sometime in the Fall season of 2022, and I'm turning it in April. Who knows what will happen even in the six months the book is being designed and printed! Will the bills pass? Will the union revote go a different way? Will Amazon sabotage contract negotiations if a union does form? Who knows! So, as much as I'm happy to update the book, I hope its core message is clear regardless of what exactly Amazon is doing at the time. Things will always change, but here's something that won't: big tech monopolies, especially Amazon's, are bad for communities, small businesses, the planet, consumers, and workers. On the other hand, small businesses, especially those that pay a living wage and treat their workers with dignity, can enrich communities in ways exactly opposite to the way that Amazon destroys them. Until Amazon's massive power, greed, and overreach are successfully broken up, its threat to communities and workers remains.

–*Danny Caine, March 15, 2022*

INTRODUCTION
WHY *HOW TO RESIST AMAZON AND WHY*

*E*very workday, every task I perform is somehow related to books. I open boxes full of them. I put them on the shelf. I order them. I return them. I hand them to customers I think will love them. I watch as a team of dedicated booksellers does all of the above alongside me. Every day I unlock the doors of the bookstore I co-own—The Raven Book Store in Lawrence, Kansas—so I can sell, discuss, and dream about books alongside my team. Every day I go to work and I'm reminded that there can be a place for independent bookstores in 21st century America. I'm reminded that independent small businesses can carve a space to earn a living and shape their communities. I'm reminded that books, and those who sell them, are resilient and beloved.

Many of us in the independent bookstore world would fight to defend the idea of The Book with a capital B. For some of us, it's hard to even talk about how we feel about The Book without getting grandiose. Some of us believe the right book can change the world. Some believe the right book can grow empathy in its reader, and that empathy can blossom into positive change. Some believe the right book can forever alter the course of the right reader's life. It's all high and mighty, but it's true. We believe in these objects and their power, and our work is to help the right books get into the right hands.

Since 1995, we've watched as Amazon has become a bigger and bigger threat to that work.

There has never been a company as big, powerful, and pervasive as Amazon. Amazon is disruptive to the ability of small businesses to stay afloat. Amazon is a continuation of the story begun when Walmart and other megastores began their rapid spread. Amazon is indeed the latest link in a chain of threats to the American retail small business, from shopping malls to chain megastores to online e-commerce giants, each acting in their own pernicious way to destroy the American downtown.

Yet Amazon is more dangerous than Walmart because it's so much bigger, and it has its hands in so many more businessesses. Amazon Web Services is a cloud computing system that provides the data infrastructure for much of the Internet, from government servers to Netflix. It's near impossible for anyone to use the Internet without Amazon's silent participation. This alone means Amazon has a gigantic impact on everyday life. Beyond that, Amazon's massive portfolio of companies and products mean Amazon has a hand in every Ring doorbell, every Whole Foods grocery purchase, every Audible audiobook, every Goodreads review, every article in the *Washington Post*, every shoe from Zappos, every stream on Twitch, plus many online advertisements and smart speakers and e-readers and TV shows. Amazon has even built its own nationwide delivery network; rather than work with USPS, UPS, and Fedex, Amazon has fashioned its own private version from the ground up, and the results are dangerous.

Amazon executives regularly downplay Amazon's size; in a PBS Frontline documentary Amazon CEO of Worldwide Commerce Jeff Wilke claims, "We're 1% of the retail sales in the world, about."[1] But what percentage of eBook sales does Amazon control? Of cloud hosting? Of online advertising? Of lobbying? Of groceries? Of online shoe sales? Of online book sales? A single company having a stake in so many different aspects of the market is dangerous. Through its Amazon Marketplace platform, Amazon acts as host for a third-party marketplace *and* a competitor on that platform. Basically, Amazon is a referee and a player in the same game, and the game is the world's largest online retail marketplace. On top of its unfair double role, Amazon charges its marketplace sellers exorbitant fees that line its pockets and make it nearly impossible for small businesses to sell on Marketplace long-term. Walmart is still a threat to American small businesses, but Walmart never did quite so *much*. It's now possible to argue that Walmart is trying to catch up to Amazon.

Amazon's impact is huge. One of the world's most valuable companies, it has caused havoc in every industry it has touched. My industry, books, happens to be the first industry at which Amazon took aim. Everybody in the book business feels Amazon's might. Booksellers feel it the most in this way: it is possible to buy the latest bestseller on Amazon for less than the *wholesale price* my bookstore pays. Let that sink in. A book that costs me $14 to put on my shelves could be for sale to *customers* on Amazon for $10. It's stunning: you can buy a book below cost and have it at your door tomorrow with free shipping. That fact alone underlies everything I do at The Raven. Even more, the cheapness of Amazon's books serves to diminish the value of all books, regardless of where they're sold.

It's so easy to buy things on Amazon, and millions of people know it. Amazon's smiling boxes sprinkle stoops across the world. Their smiling vans double park on blocks in countless cities and their smiling semis haul down countless interstates. The massive shipping network required to get that box to you so cheap and so fast is a strain on the environment, not to mention unsafe to its drivers and customers. The warehouses that feed that shipping network have injury rates high above industry average and are highly susceptible to outbreaks of deadly diseases like COVID-19. Ring home cameras make it far too easy to feed video data to police departments. Amazon Web Services earns lots of money, including from violent agencies like ICE. Amazon makes things easy; they don't necessarily make them right.

Some may try to attribute the explosion of Amazon's reach to Jeff Bezos's business brilliance. However, even if Bezos had a profitable idea at the right time, literal billions in tax breaks and government benefits have helped Amazon rise to the pinnacle it occupies today. Nowhere is this better demonstrated than the HQ2 search, a contest for cities to compete to host a second Amazon headquarters. Cities fell over themselves to offer Amazon the biggest possible portfolios of tax breaks and corporate welfare. It was a display of just how far governments would go to subsidize a trillion-dollar company. In 2018, Amazon made over $11 billion in profits and paid no federal income tax.

Every decision Amazon makes causes shockwaves in the industries that Amazon has—to borrow Silicon Valley parlance—*disrupted*. TV, shoes, groceries, web traffic, home security, e-commerce, books, e-books, audiobooks. They've all had to scramble to adapt to the force of the company founded by Jeff Bezos, the world's richest man. The book-related decisions Amazon makes send ripples across the entire publishing industry like a boulder tossed into a pond. Maybe that's too peaceful. Amazon's effect on the book world is like a video you'd see in high school chemistry class: not a boulder tossed into a pond but a chunk of pure sodium that explodes the instant it touches water. Amazon accounts for a majority of all book sales in the United States. Booksellers, authors, libraries, publishers, wholesalers, agents, authors, designers—we all feel it. Amazon holds sway over every aspect of books and publishing. Again, Amazon, one single retailer, accounts for a majority of all books sold in the United States. That alone should be cause for concern. And that's just the book industry. Even more concerning is Amazon's effect on individual liberties, shipping infrastructure, workers' rights, and the environment.

We must resist Amazon.

Amazon was founded to disrupt the bookselling business. Rather than a small brick-and-mortar store with, say, 25,000 books, Amazon was, at its start, an online-only bookstore with millions of titles. Unlike so many people in the book industry, Bezos didn't get into bookselling out of a passion for reading or literacy. According to biographer Brad Stone, Bezos picked books because "they were pure commodities; a copy of a book in one store was identical to the same book carried in another."[2] Further, "most important, there were three million books in print worldwide, far more than a Barnes & Noble or a Borders superstore could ever stock."[3] Until Jeff Bezos came along, the book industry was built on curation; Amazon disrupted that model by simply selling everything. Amazon has since repeated this "everything store" model with countless other industries, but books were the first target, and one of the hardest hit.

Disruption doesn't automatically equal progress. Amazon puts my business—and countless others like it—at risk. If we're put out of business by Amazon's disruption, it means more than just an empty storefront. A small business, especially one that pays a living wage and otherwise treats its workers well, serves its community in many ways beyond the sale of retail goods. Communities are threatened if small businesses can no longer thrive thanks to Amazon's reach. Even if Amazon doesn't put bookstores out of business, it shrinks their market share, leaving fewer resources to compensate workers. In other words, Amazon makes it harder for small businesses to pay that living wage. If the world's biggest retailer of books is working to devalue books, then working in the production and selling of books is less lucrative. The emotional joy of selling books is often viewed as a perk of the job, but the joy of selling books is not legal tender that you can use on groceries or medical treatment.

The Amazon fight isn't the first time independent bookstores and small businesses have taken on larger competition in an effort to stake a claim. During Walmart's expansion years, "shop local" movements sprang up across the country. Events like Small Business Saturday, Record Store Day, and Independent Bookstore Day aim to celebrate small businesses and their contributions. The craft beer explosion represents a successful small business resistance in the face of industry-dominating titans, though monopolies are still fighting to overtake that industry, too. The bookstores-vs-corporate-titans fight even reached the courtroom: in the late 1990s, the American Booksellers Association sued Borders and Barnes & Noble over predatory pricing methods similar to Amazon's today.

The Raven Book Store still feels the remnants of the indies-vs-megastore fight: from the cash register at our original location, you could see across the street to the empty building that housed a Borders Books & Music from 1997-2011. There's a bit of comfort in knowing we're still open while the Borders is shuttered. So why can't bookstores just sue Amazon the way we sued the big chains in 1998? Simply put: we can't afford to. Amazon is much bigger and much more powerful than the big book chains ever were. There's also evidence that Amazon is more willing to fight dirty. So we must find new ways to resist Amazon's growth and influence.

If Amazon is allowed to grow unchecked, it's hard to know what exactly they'll try to do. Jeff Bezos has said his ultimate goal is to colonize space. If Amazon continues to bulldoze everything in its path, he very well may achieve that goal. But here's what else he'll achieve: the destruction of countless American small businesses. The end of the ability to spend an hour quietly browsing an independent bookstore. The shuttering of grocery stores and co-ops. If Amazon grows unchecked, your neighbor's house might be able to automatically call the cops on you because that house's doorbell has flagged you as suspicious in a facial recognition database. If Amazon grows unchecked and its web services hold up more of the Internet's backbone, might this single company have too much sway over what gets said or posted online? Finally, If Amazon, America's second-biggest employer, has its way, the resurgent U.S. labor movement is all but over. Before we let Amazon become as big as it wants to be, we must investigate what it stands for.

To help people investigate what Amazon stands for, I've written this book. The book world is very good at talking amongst itself about Amazon's effect. I decided it was time to bring that discussion to our customers, first through The Raven's Twitter account, then through a zine called *How to Resist Amazon and Why*, and now through this book. It is an entry point, a beginner's guide to resisting Amazon. There is much more to know and understand about Amazon than what is contained in these pages, but I've included suggestions for further reading for those who wish to dive deeper. This book is intended for those who are beginning to feel uneasy about Amazon. Hopefully it can serve as a guide for how to unplug from this dangerous company, as well as a brief summary of the compelling reasons to do so.

Half the chapters in *How to Resist Amazon and Why* build a case against Amazon around central themes like "The Environment" or "Jobs" or "Shipping." In between each of these case-against-Amazon chapters is a narrative interlude, mainly from the perspective of my small business. These interludes, hopefully, are quiet demonstrations of the power and potential of places like The Raven Book Store. They're meant to empower and advocate for independent businesses, but also to demonstrate a little bit of what's at stake if Amazon makes it harder for all of us to flourish. Finally, the book concludes with a chapter outlining concrete steps you can take to resist Amazon.

Despite the title of the book, this is about more than one company. I've framed this book around Amazon because Amazon is the most powerful, effective, and ruthless practitioner of a new kind of commerce, but many others are trying to learn from Amazon's playbook. This new commerce is more than one company selling a lot of books—it's a fundamental revision of how we view privacy. Of how we view a business's role in American society. Of the limits on the power of a single business. Of our environment. In some ways, of what it means to be human. Amazon's thinking represents a shift in the American way of life, and if you ask me, it's a shift worth resisting. I am resolute in the idea that being human means more than being a source of data with which companies can sell you things. Being human is about things that can't be measured in clicks, data, or money. If you ask me, we should resist companies that want to tear down those ways of being human. Good news: if you've read this far, you're already on your way.

INTERLUDE 1

A LETTER TO JEFF BEZOS FROM A SMALL BOOKSTORE IN THE MIDDLE OF THE COUNTRY

Jeff Bezos

CEO and President

Amazon

Seattle, WA

October 22, 2019

Dear Jeff:

Last Wednesday a customer bought a stack of books from us. Right before he left, he asked me, "what parts of your business are affected by Amazon?" I blurted out, "every part." I had never articulated this before, but it's true. I know I'm not alone in saying this, and not just among bookstores, either. Your business has an unfair impact on every retail small business in America. I'm writing to you to try to illustrate just how many people your business affects in a negative way.

Let's start with books, because that's where we overlap and books are my bread and butter. Correct me if I'm wrong, but it certainly seems like the book part of your business is modeled like this: sell books at a loss to hook people into Prime subscriptions, Kindles, Alexas, and other higher-margin products. While this strategy has worked really well for you, it's totally disrupted everything about the book business, making a low-margins business even tighter. Most dismayingly to us, your book business has devalued the book itself. People expect hardcovers to be 15 bucks and paperbacks to be under 10. Those margins are a nightmare for our bottom line, of course, but they also cheapen the idea of the capital-B Book. There's already enough happening to cheapen the idea of truth, research, and careful storytelling. We're alarmed to see the world's biggest book retailer reflecting that frightening cultural shift by de-valuing books.

This isn't just about business competition to us. We wish it were! We like business competition, we think it's healthy. But the way you've set things up makes it impossible to compete with you. Often the tech and e-commerce world brags about "disrupting" old ways of doing things with new, sleeker, more efficient tricks. But we refuse to be a quaint old way of doing things, and we are not ripe for disruption. We're not relics. We're community engines. We create free programming. We donate gift certificates to charity silent auctions. We partner with libraries and arts organizations. That stuff might seem small to someone aiming to colonize outer space, but to us and our community it's huge. Our booksellers are farmers, authors, activists, artists, board members, city council representatives. For so many places, the loss of an indie bookstore would mean the loss of a community force. If your retail experiment disrupts us into extinction you're not threatening quaint old ways of doing things. You're threatening communities.

When I taught high school English, we did a business letter unit. Part of what I taught was to make sure every business letter has some kind of request so it's not a waste of time or paper. So, what to request from you? Some of my peers want to break your company up. Some of them want to nationalize it. Some of them want it wiped off the earth. I see where they're all coming from, but I don't think that's what I'm after today (though, if I'm being perfectly frank, breaking your company up seems like an increasingly good idea). I could also request you stop profiting off ICE's violence, stop enabling counterfeit merchandise, stop fostering a last-mile shipping system that causes injury and death, stop gentrifying our cities, stop contributing to the police state with your doorbell cameras, stop driving your warehouse workers to injury and busting up their unionizing attempts, or so many other things. Perhaps I could just request an explanation of why this chaos and violence is apparently so essential to your strategy.

Or maybe I could request a leveling of the playing field. Small business owners are led to believe that if their idea is good enough, they can grow their business enough to make sure the jobs they provide are good, paying a living wage and providing benefits. Maybe they could even create more of their good jobs as their business grows. Yet your company is so big, so disruptive, so dominant, that it's severely skewed the ability for us to do that. I think a big part of leveling the playing field would mean fair pricing on your part. For our part, we try to level things by being really good at what we do, and really loud. So we use our platform to try to teach people what's at stake as your company increases its influence and market share. I think it's starting to work. I get the feeling that we're seeing chips in Amazon's armor. Whenever we share stuff like this, it seems to resonate with our audience. Maybe someday you'll hear what we have to say. Maybe we can talk about it over pie and coffee at Ladybird Diner across the street, my treat. I'd love to show you around a vibrant community anchored by small businesses, here in Kansas, here on earth. Maybe it'll help you realize that some things don't need to be disrupted.

Sincerely,

Danny Caine, Owner

Raven Book Store

Lawrence, KS

CHAPTER 1

ON AMAZON AND THE BOOK INDUSTRY

Right now, as I write this in February 2019, bestseller *Where the Crawdads Sing* is on sale at Amazon for $9.59. If I were to order that book directly from the publisher for The Raven's shelves, I'd have to write the publisher a check for $14.04 per copy. Amazon is selling this book for almost $5 less than my *cost*. That means if I were to sell this book at Amazon's price, I might as well just hand the customer a $5 bill from the register. The Raven sells this book, like any other book, for the price printed on the cover. *Crawdads* has it right there on the inside flap of the dust jacket: $26. How do customers feel when they see me trying to sell an incredibly popular book for $16.41 more than the price they can get it for online? Amazon's dramatic book discounts are just one way they wreak havoc on the book industry. Since its founding in 1995, Amazon has increasingly bent the book industry to its will. Amazon has affected the way books are designed, distributed, printed, and sold, and their efforts to do so have devalued the capital-B Book. Amazon's influence on the publishing industry is so vast that it affects even the smallest decisions made in the smallest bookstores.

As a co-owner of a small independent bookstore I feel Amazon's impact every day. Business competition is one thing, but it's hard to argue that the way Amazon looms over every aspect of our business counts as fair competition. Most books come with the prices printed on the outside; our narrow margin (generally around 40% of the cost of each book) is calculated from the book's printed price. That 40% is lower than the margin on many other retail goods, typically 50% or higher. Sometimes that higher margin comes from the fact that a store can raise the price of an item in order to better meet sales projections. That's why bookstores like to sell greeting cards: you can set your own margin on a greeting card so they're technically more profitable than books. But a bookstore can't really raise the price of a book; if we charged $30 for a $25 book, the customer could point at the $25 printed right on the back and, rightly, ask us what the heck we're trying to do. Lowering the price of a book isn't an option, either, as that would cut into a margin that's already smaller than average. That small margin is where we get, among other things, employee salaries. I don't know about other bookstore owners, but I can't in good conscience make decisions that lead to lower pay for my workers. So we're basically stuck with the price the publisher sets. In some countries, there are even laws that prevent cutting book prices. But in America, independent bookstores and small businesses have no protection from the threat of Amazon's pricing practices. (Before I'm accused of being elitist or trying to prevent people without means from accessing books, let me say I'm a staunch advocate for public libraries and used bookstores. Both are better ways of getting cheap books than buying cut-price new books on Amazon).

Unlike nearly every independent bookstore, Amazon can and does drastically cut prices on books, ignoring the publisher's printed price. Amazon can do this because they don't need to make money on books, especially bestsellers. They can offer *Crawdads* as a loss leader because of the staggering array of profitable revenue streams in their portfolio. Much of Amazon's revenue doesn't even come from their retail business at all: their server company Amazon Web Services (AWS) is the backbone of much of the content and advertising that appears on the Internet. Internet backboning has a much better profit margin than retail goods, so Amazon can rely on AWS profits to let their retail arm "disrupt" the retail world. "Disrupt," translated from Silcon Valley-ese into English, means "fuck up irreparably." In recent years, according to new findings from the Institute for Local Self Reliance, third-party seller fees account for an even bigger slice of Amazon's revenue than AWS. According to ILSR's "Amazon's Monopoly Toll Road" report, revenue from third-party seller fees grew faster than Amazon's own retail sales and faster than its Prime membership program. They even outpaced Amazon Web Services, pulling in twice as much as the server division's 61 billion in sales.[4] Trust me: anybody who's only selling books isn't talking about numbers like that.

An independent bookstore does not have a supremely profitable web hosting service in its portfolio, nor do we have a chokehold on millions of small business owners, forcing them to pay us exorbitant user fees. If we can't make money selling books, we can't make money. 80-90% of what we sell are books. We open bookstores because we love books, and our ability to continue doing that is being threatened by a big tech company's experiment in disrupting our industry. The promise of the American small business is to find a niche doing something you're passionate about. If that niche meets some kind of demand, or serves some kind of community, you can (allegedly) make a living with a small enterprise you've built. Amazon's apparent use of other revenue streams to enable below-cost retail pricing is threatening the promise of American small business.

Is this legal? Well, yes and no. If Amazon's endgame were to lower prices to drive competitors out of business, then raise prices once they'd cornered the market, then no. This is called predatory pricing and it's illegal under U.S. antitrust laws. But the burden of proof is very high for predatory pricing cases, and few if any are ever proven in court. Plus, as discussed in a later chapter, U.S. antitrust laws have been obsessed with keeping prices low for the past 40 years. If a company's actions, no matter how predatory, are keeping prices low for customers, it's highly unlikely the government will intervene.

•   •   •

While we're on the subject of book pricing, let's dive in a little further. Here's how book pricing and profit usually works. We'll use this book as an example. This book has a sticker price of $14.95. When Microcosm Publishing sells this book directly to a bookstore, Microcosm generally gets something like 54% of that $14.95, or roughly $8.07. When the book sells, the bookstore keeps the other $6.88 and uses it to pay its bills, employees, and maybe even eke out a few cents of profit. In my publishing contract for this book, which is fairly typical, 15% of Microcosm's $8.07 goes to me, the author. So if you bought this book at full price, thank you for your contribution of $1.21 to the Danny Caine author fund. After my cut, Microcosm then gets $6.85 for printing and marketing the book, as well as paying its employees and bills. Since this is a small press book, you're contributing to the local economy of

Portland, Oregon and Cleveland, Ohio by helping Microcosm, a small business, provide jobs and economic activity. If you bought it from a local bookstore, same thing for whatever economy that bookstore is contributing to. You also contributed a small part to whomever printed the book, and the people who moved it from Microcosm's warehouse to the bookstore. Your $14.95 was spread across lots of different companies, people, and local economies. This split of the publishing pie, like so much of the book world, is something Amazon is working very hard to disrupt.

Say a customer wants to buy the new novel from bestselling crime novelist Dean Koontz. They could get it on Amazon. At one point, they could've gotten it from a brick and mortar bookstore inside the mall at Columbus Circle. They could download it to their Kindle. They could download it from Audible. If they liked it, they could post about it on Goodreads. All perfectly normal ways to interact with a book. And in this case, all ways to give money to the world's richest man.

Every one of these ways to engage with a new Koontz book benefits Amazon. This isn't surprising. But there's a wrinkle in the Dean Koontz case: Dean Koontz is now signed to a deal where an Amazon-owned imprint is publishing his books, too. No matter how a customer buys a new Dean Koontz book, even if they buy it from an independent bookstore, the money goes to Amazon. Any new book by Dean Koontz is edited, printed, published, marketed, and sold by a single company. He appears to know this—he's quoted in the *Wall Street Journal* saying, "We had seven or eight offers, but Amazon offered the most complete marketing plan, and that was the deciding factor."[5] The plan is complete because Amazon can do every single thing that needs to be done for this book. One book, one company at every step. Traditionally, a publisher and a bookseller and a wholesaler and a shipping company are four different entities that all have a hand in selling a book. It's four different companies that can make money off of a single title. More slices of the pie. But with Amazon-exclusive deals like Koontz's, the pie isn't even sliced. Koontz gets his percentage of royalties, and Amazon gets the rest of the entire pie. Even shipping the book from place to place might happen entirely in Amazon-controlled trucks and planes. The part about multiple small businesses and local economies getting a slice of the price of that book? Gone. After giving Dean Koontz a tiny slice, Amazon eats the rest. Certainly, Amazon would love to do this with more authors. One notable example of Amazon's success at recruiting authors is Colleen Hoover, whose popularity on TikTok has sent her to the top of bestseller lists. One of her most recent books, *Reminders of Him*, even appeared on the American Booksellers Association's Indie Bookstore Bestseller list at the end of January 2022. Trouble is, *Reminders of Him* is published by Montlake, Amazon Publishing's romance imprint. Every copy of *Reminders of Him* that moved through indie bookstores actually lined the pockets of the company working to destroy indie bookstores. I imagine some folks at Amazon were pretty thrilled about that.

Aside from fewer slices of the financial pie, one company controlling everything about a book's life cycle could pose a theoretical danger too: the consolidation of power and influence, especially in regards to books, rarely leads to freer expression. If one company has control over every step of publishing and selling a book, it's natural that the single company will bend whatever's in that book to fit its purposes. The same way a totalitarian government silences dissenting voices, a totalitarian publishing industry will silence any voice that doesn't serve its algorithms. One example of Amazon's massive growth having a dampening effect on free speech can be found in China: in recent years, Amazon has disabled comments and reviews on many books on their Chinese site, in one instance going so far as to only allow five-star reviews on a book by Chinese president Xi Jinping.[6] A free and robust exchange of different perspectives and voices can't thrive if one company with totalitarian tendencies oversees every aspect of every book's production, editing, and distribution.

All of this, from Amazon's potentially predatory pricing to their book consolidation, puts a tremendous amount of pressure on indie bookstores. People often flinch at the full price when we tell them how much a book costs. Some even tell us just how much cheaper it is at Amazon. Another thing we hear all the time: that a customer *swears* they've seen a paperback version "online" of a book that's only available in hardcover. Here's how paperbacks and hardcovers work for businesses that play by the rules: in America, publishers release cheaper paperback versions of books only when the expensive hardcovers have stopped selling. When a book like *Where the Crawdads Sing* becomes a runaway hit in hardcover, the publisher has no need to put out a cheaper paperback version, because the hardcover is still making money. This, understandably, is frustrating to customers (it ended up taking 959 days—just over two and a half years—for the paperback version of *Crawdads* to be released). Still, a vast majority of paperbacks are released within a year of their hardcover versions. But those bestsellers are tricky because they can run for 2 or 3 years, or even forever, in the expensive hardcover version.

Often, paperback versions of books appear earlier in Europe and those paperbacks end up on the Amazon Marketplace in the United States. Publishers also circulate draft paperback copies of books in advance of the hardcover releases to booksellers and reviewers to generate buzz. Part of the agreements we enter with publishers is a promise that we won't sell these European paperbacks or advance copies to our customers; doing so would lead to penalties with our vendors. But here's the thing: we still see customers all the time who say "I swear I saw the paperback online." And they did. Amazon makes it far too easy for third-party sellers to sell European paperbacks or advance copies of books that are still available only in hardcover for those of us who play by the rules. "Why not just break the rules and sell the advance copies?" you say. Well, that might lead us to lose our publisher accounts, and if we can't get books directly from publishers, we make less money on books. Bookstores and publishers need to work together for bookstores to succeed. Plus, a small bookstore doesn't have enough leverage to walk away from a fight with a publisher unscathed. Amazon, on the other hand, has all the leverage in the world: According to the *New York Times*'s David Streitfeld, Amazon "has as much as two-thirds of the market for new and used books through its own platform and such subsidiaries as Abebooks.com."[7] What publisher would be okay with losing most of their sales to a dispute over European paperbacks and advance copies for sale? So, ultimately, the impression Amazon gives our customers is that Amazon can offer something we can't.

A similar occurrence—the false appearance that Amazon can sell a product we can't—happened in the lead-up to the release of Margaret Atwood's *The Testaments*. *The Testaments* was a hugely anticipated book, the much buzzed-about sequel to *The Handmaid's Tale*. With high profile releases like this, bookstores have to sign an affidavit before they can even order their copies. The affidavit states that the store swears not to display the copies of the book before the on-sale date. This one was particularly strict, saying, "you must ensure that the book is stored in a monitored and locked, secured area and not placed on the selling floor prior to the on-sale date." What happens if we break the agreement? According to the affidavit:

> "any store that violates the restrictions found in this Agreement will be subject to the following: (i) we will be liable for any and all damages incurred as a result of such Violations, (ii) PRH may require that resupply, in whole or in part, to the violating store of The Testaments by Margaret Atwood, be withheld. Furthermore, we acknowledge and agree that any such violation may cause irreparable harm to PRH and the author and that monetary damages may be inadequate to compensate for violations and that, in addition to any other remedies that may be available, at law, in equity or otherwise, PRH and/or the author may be entitled to obtain injunctive relief, without the necessity of proving actual damages or posting any bond."

So, if we break the affidavit, we have some scary legalese waiting for us. Essentially, if we're caught selling a book before publication date we face consequences like delayed shipments of other big books, which would cause us to lose crucial first-week sales. We could even lose our account with that publisher, or, according to the affidavit, owe them damages. These consequences are scary, but it's not difficult for us to just not ship or set out the book before pub date. We make this promise all the time. Everyone else does too. But this time, things would be different.

The first any of us heard of it was one tiny post in a private Indie Bookstore Facebook group on Tuesday, September 3. A new bookstore owner had preordered Margaret Atwood's *The Testaments* on Amazon. This was before she owned a bookstore, before she had been indoctrinated in the industry-wide grudge we all hold against the company we sometimes call, simply, A. The fact that she ordered *The Testaments* on Amazon didn't upset us, though. What upset us was the fact that she got it on Tuesday, September 3, a full week before its publication date. This was bad news. I went to bed that night hoping it was an isolated incident. It wasn't.

Turns out, that bookseller's lone early arrival was symptomatic of a much bigger problem. It's unclear how many copies of *The Testaments* shipped out early, but it was a lot. Though they didn't name their source, *The Guardian* seemed to think 800 copies went out. People excitedly posted on social media about their early copies. Indie Bookstores started to make noise, and for good reason.

Amazon sending books out early like this was bad in many ways: first, it broke the rules. Every retailer who wanted to sell *The Testaments* had to sign that fairly intense affidavit swearing to keep the books under literal lock and key until 9/10/19. Second, the early release gave news outlets de facto permission to run early reviews and excerpts so the mystique and mystery about what happened in the book was gone. Third, Amazon's early release gave the impression that people can get a book faster if they order it from Amazon instead of their slower, more expensive indie bookstore. We already fight to convince people to spend more for books; now, it seemed, we'd have to fight to make people wait longer to get those books, too.

All we heard from Atwood's publisher were vague variations on the fact that things were being taken care of. The book sold well for us, but it wasn't, as expected, Fall's biggest book. I have to wonder if the flubbed release deflated the excitement about the book. Regardless, *The Testaments* will always remind me of a time when Amazon got away with something its smaller competitors would've been severely punished for.

And that's the thing—Amazon is too big to punish. In a big publisher vs. Amazon fight, all leverage goes to Amazon because the big publishers need Amazon. Like any industry, book publishing is dominated by huge companies. More than half of U.S. book sales happen on Amazon, and the top five publishers (Penguin Random House, HarperCollins, Simon & Schuster, Hachette, and Macmillan) account for, by some estimates, 80% of book sales. A fight between a Big Five publisher and Amazon is bound to send shockwaves through the industry, but Amazon's majority of all book sales gives them the leverage.

In 2014, Amazon got into a dispute about ebook pricing with big-five conglomerate publisher Hachette. Both companies wanted the last word in the prices of Hachette's ebooks. More important than the details of the dispute are the lengths Amazon went to to flex their muscle: Amazon delayed shipments on all Hachette books and hid Hachette preorder pages, certainly sinking sales of Hachette books.[8] More than 300 authors wrote a letter encouraging "Amazon in the strongest possible terms to stop harming the livelihood of the authors on whom it has built its business."[9] The dispute was eventually settled, with Amazon granting Hachette the power to set ebook prices, but the damage was done. Amazon successfully showed its massive power to disrupt the publishing industry as a whole. But it's impossible for most publishers to walk away from a vendor that accounts for most of U.S. book sales. Many publishers feel this—ambivalence (or hatred) towards Amazon, coupled with a reluctant acceptance that you can't lose the sales Amazon offers. To me, this is a sign of a company that is too big. It has an entire industry grasped in its fist.

These are just the big book-industry stories. Seemingly every day something happens that reminds indie bookstores of Amazon's huge power. During the first Senate impeachment trial of Donald Trump, news dropped that former national security adviser John Bolton had not only written a book, but the book contained bombshell revelations about the Ukraine Affair. By this point, the only things independent bookstores had heard about Bolton's book were rumors of a huge book deal. But as soon as the *New York Times* published their report, a preorder page was live on Amazon.com. When all we knew were vaporous rumors, Bolton's publisher had already given Amazon a title, cover, ISBN, and synopsis: everything they needed to start collecting money. In a breakneck news cycle packed with bombshell tell-alls, the first 24 hours after revelations appear are absolutely crucial for making money off of these books. Ravenbookstore.com automatically pulls data from Ingram, the industry's largest wholesaler. The fact that Amazon had this data before Ingram had automatically sent it to my website (or any other indie bookstore's website) means Amazon was given priority in learning about this book's existence. While I could've scraped Amazon for the data, adding it to my site would've been a labor-intensive manual process and every minute counts in the breakneck news cycle. The information finally made it to Ingram 3 days after Amazon had it. We didn't get any initial preorders. But it's not just preorders Amazon is "disrupting;" they even have their sights set on things as universal as how books look.

Amazon, and its massive market share, is even changing the way books are designed. According to *Vulture*, "At a time when half of all book purchases in the U.S. are made on Amazon—and many of those on mobile—the first job of a book cover, after gesturing at the content inside, is to look great in miniature."[10] If you've noticed that there are a lot of novels with bold blocky titles over vibrant patterned backgrounds recently, it's because those covers look great on a computer screen. Writing for *Vulture,* Margot Boyer-Dry writes, "If books have design eras, we're in an age of statement wallpaper and fatty text. We have the Internet to thank."[11] Amazon knows the power of a good Amazon-friendly cover design, and it employs that knowledge to great results. *Publishers Weekly* analyzed results of a Fall 2019 study by the Codex Group measuring how book covers entice customers to browse. More than 50 book covers were shown to upwards of 4,000 consumers alongside a "read more" button. A click on "read more" counted as a browse. Eight of the top ten most browsed books were Amazon-published titles with Amazon-designed covers.[12] They're reshaping the look of books, and they know what they're doing.

The smallest decision by Amazon is enough to send all of publishing into a panic. According to an editorial in *N+1*, "Amazon remains capable of crippling the industry and upending its practices with little more than an algorithmic tweak."[13] Examples of this are rampant, but here's one: In the lead-up to the crucial fourth quarter in 2019, Amazon all of a sudden started placing orders much lower than the previous year's orders for the same month.[14] They blamed capacity issues. One independent publisher said if Amazon orders don't rise to what has been typical ordering patterns in past years within two weeks, "we [could] lose the entire holiday season." For people in the retail business, the holiday season is when profits happen, if they happen at all. Losing a holiday season means increased debt, letting employees go, and making difficult adjustments for the entire following year. Here's an independent business in fear of losing the most important time of year simply based on one decision made by one retailer. This panic echoed across many of the same types of businesses. The case of Amazon and the book business is the case of Amazon getting too big, and its growth doesn't appear to be slowing.

One more important way Amazon's dominance affects book shopping: the experience of shopping for books on Amazon simply isn't good. To shop for books on Amazon is to sift through a mess of fake listings, bootleg books, scams, and paid placements, at times making the act of finding a specific edition nearly impossible. Amazon's search results may be so bad as to be criminal: in December 2021, a coalition of labor unions filed an FTC complaint alleging that Amazon "is unlawfully deceiving millions of consumers by failing to "clearly and conspicuously" disclose which of its search engine results are paid advertisements rather than 'organic' search results."[15] The FTC, headed by vocal Amazon critic Lina Khan, will likely take the complaint quite seriously. The sloppiness of Amazon's book buying experience isn't just bad for the consumer and possibly illegal; it might be bad for the book industry as a whole.

In December 2021, *New York Times* technology reporter David Streitfeld went deep on how exactly book shopping on Amazon is so terrible. Streitfeld talks to one author who found copies of his own books, mislabeled with publication dates in the 17th century, on sale for $900+ for no apparent reason. Turns out, fake-dating book listings gets a book a separate page, which might goose that vendor's rankings or placements on search pages.[16] Despite it making Amazon more difficult to navigate, and increasing the odds that customers will get something they didn't order, this kind of trickery is widespread. For a few days in January 2022, the page for *Gratitude* by Oliver Sacks displayed a button directing to a $74.99 paperback option, despite a paperback version never having been released. When I clicked on the paperback button, I found not Oliver Sacks's posthumous book, but rather a $75 vibrator. This is good for the sketchy third-party seller, but of course bad for the customer (pardon the pun, but Oliver Sacks and a sex toy have different . . . vibes). A lot of this manipulation is a bold-faced attempt to trick customers into buying the wrong thing. These Marketplace mega-sellers don't want to sell you the right thing, they want to sell you *their* thing, and Amazon is slow to stop it. One notorious example of this, as explained by Streitfeld, is the University Press phenomenon. "University Press" is a mysterious entity, certainly not a university press, that publishes low-quality books about people who have notable biographies out at the moment. One example is University Press's *Dave Grohl: The Biography*, which University Press paid to promote alongside Dave Grohl's very popular real book *The Storyteller*. Because University Press paid to promote it, their crummy bootleg version can appear first in the search results, scamming people into buying a book written in what Streitfeld calls "Almost English," rather than the legit book they might be looking for.[17] As I write this in February 2022, an Amazon search for "1619 Project" yields these results, in order:*

1. *The 1619 Project Book: A Brief History of the 1619 Project* by University Reads

2. *The 1619 Project Book: A Brief History of the 1619 Project* by University Press, complete with an orange "Bestseller" flag

---

* A May 2022 double-check shows the proper book first, which possibly indicates its publisher paying to resolve the University Press Problem. Also worth noting with the May 2022 search, is that above the book sits an ad for ultra-right wing publisher Regnery, who is also paying to be right there.

3. *The 1619 Project*, #1 the bestselling actual book edited by Nikole Hannah-Jones

We've been taught to trust the first result on any search page, and Amazon knows this, steering us to whomever paid to promote their book the most (in this case, whoever the hell "University Reads" and "University Press" are). Just imagine a kid asking a well-meaning grandma for "the new Dave Grohl book," only to unwrap an "almost-English" bootleg on Christmas morning. University Press doesn't care, and neither does Amazon. They both get their money.

Artist Angie Waller's hybrid nonfiction/art book *Grifting the Amazon* is a valuable look at how exactly these shoddy self-published books get made. In *Grifting*, Angie Waller describes her process of becoming something a bit like University Press. The book is Waller's behind-the-scenes story of composing and putting out these half-baked books. The first step in Waller's sketchy publishing journey is taking a Skillshare class promoting Kindle publishing as "passive income." Then, as the class instructs, Waller mulls whether to use a pseudonym, since the Kindle system requires "no verification that the name of an author [is] connected to a real identity. Any name or fictional brand could be listed as the book's author".[18] This explains why these books come from places like University Press—the names sound legit to a distracted or inexperienced buyer, and Amazon just doesn't care what you call yourself when you self-publish a book. Next, as Waller's class instructed, she pulls titles from websites that aggregate Google searches. This ensures the searchability buzzworthiness of her books. A few of the titles she chooses include *How to Find a Friend, Be a Good Friend, and Delete a Friend*; *How to Tell if Someone is Listening to You in Your House;* and the strangely poetic *What Does the Bible Say About Word Finds?*, the last of which you can still buy on Amazon. Once Waller has titles, she hires overseas ghostwriters through Upwork.com, where people around the world get gig-economy freelance jobs ("Almost English" might be a little on the nose, as it turns out). Freelance rates on Upwork.com go as low as the bargain-basement 1 cent per word, in part because there's no quality control or editorial guidance on assignments like these Amazon content-farm books (for contrast, a high-profile well-edited magazine piece can draw up to $1 per word). Finally, without any edits and without checking for plagiarism, Waller uploads the Upwork-ghostwritten books to the Kindle system and, voila, the book is for sale.

In composing these books and assembling *Grifting the Amazon*, Waller runs into all kinds of weirdness on the other side of the Kindle Industrial Complex. There are bootleg authors who trade positive reviews on each other's books to make them appear more legit. There is evidence the writers are not only hiring ghostwriters for their books but also for the reviews of their books. There is evidence that a huge empire of self-published pet guides is actually one person hiring cheap ghostwriters. There's a vast array of the crappiest possible books, like *Safe Water Fasting* and *12 Amazon Tips: How to Contact Amazon By Phone By Mail How To Save Hundereds* [sic] *Bucks*. Waller even alleges that the random jacked-up prices on marketplace books are no accident, but rather a way to launder money. Waller's books remain for sale on Amazon, sometimes, inexplicably for hundreds of dollars. Presumably, Waller's process is also how University Press books and their ilk end up all over Amazon's search results. The whole thing is so dystopian, and it perfectly explains why Amazon's online bookstore is a complete mess.

The decrease in Amazon's book-shopping quality has real effects on what gets published and how. Valancourt is a small press that made their name reissuing out-of-print horror classics, bringing influential and important works to new audiences in high-quality scholarly editions. But Amazon's algorithm makes it nearly impossible for a customer to guarantee that they're getting a specific edition of a book. Valancourt's lovingly produced reissues are lumped together with bad bootlegs and print-on-demand versions, often leading customers to leave bad reviews of Valancourt's books, even though *they never actually got a Valancourt book*. Because their reissue editions got swallowed up and hidden by Amazon's sketchy algorithms, Valancourt publisher James Jenkins says, "We've largely stopped producing scholarly editions of 18th- and 19th-century texts."[19] Valancourt isn't the only publisher curtailing reissue programs because of Amazon's algorithmic obfuscation. In her newsletter *Notes from a Small Press*, Belt Publishing founder Anne Trubek writes,

For a few years, Belt republished classics in the public domain. I adored doing these reissues, and would love to do more, more, more of them. But they didn't sell very well, in no small part because they are impossible to find on Amazon. Various editions for the same title get smushed together under the same listing, so someone looking for our version of Charles Chesnutt's *Marrow of Tradition* will just be shown another, probably crappier version by another seller, unable to choose which edition they prefer.[20]

As a bookseller, trust me: not all editions of old books are created equal. For every lovingly assembled Norton or Oxford (or Belt or Valancourt) edition, there are dozens of shitty print-on-demand cash grabs scrambling to rob you of your money through bad algorithms. This isn't just bad for consumers, it's bad for literature. The sloppiness of Amazon's bookstore, and their refusal to fix it, is actively preventing people from protecting and carrying on literary legacies.

Ultimately, Amazon touches and "disrupts" nearly every aspect of the book industry. Traditionally accepted ideas like book pricing, book design, and laydown dates have less credence due to Amazon's dominance and ambitions. Amazon's dominance is way beyond simple industry traditions, though—its size and monopolizing market share are now shaping what exactly gets written, printed, and read. In 2013, anti-monopoly scholar Barry Lynn wrote in *Harpers* that, "a single private company has captured the ability to dictate terms to the people who publish our books, and hence to the people who write and read our books."[21] Now, nearly ten years later, Amazon's stranglehold on the book industry has only gotten worse.

One quick addendum before we move on from Amazon and the book industry, for a little bit of hope: starting in 2015, Amazon started building a chain of physical bookstores. An Amazon Books bookstore is a weird place, organized not by section or other logic, but by review score and algorithm. Combined with the chilly atmosphere, it made for an unsettling retail experience. Still, their arrival and eventual expansion to 24 physical bookstores made many bookstore people nervous. After all, we had figured out ways to dodge and maneuver around them as an online behemoth, but an actual outpost in our neighborhoods was a different thing entirely. When Amazon Books announced a plan to open across the street from Nashville's beloved Parnassus Books, Margaret Renkl took to the *New York Times* to write an opinion piece in praise of Parnassus. Well, here's the good news: thousands of independent bookstores survived the brunt of the Covid-19 pandemic, but Amazon Books did not. On March 2, 2022, *Reuters* announced that Amazon was closing all of its physical bookstore locations. It's a small win, as the bookstores were never the threat that the online monopoly was and still is, but it's a win nonetheless.

INTERLUDE 2
ON SMALL BUSINESS AND POLITICS

*T*n March 2020, Christian Smalls, a process assistant at Amazon's JFK8 fulfillment center on Long Island, was concerned about how little Amazon was protecting its workers from the COVID-19 pandemic raging across the world.[22] He, along with other employees at the center, began calling for protective measures. Their demands were not outrageous: they wanted access to masks and hand sanitizer and paid time off while the center was deep-cleaned. They alleged there had already been ten positive cases at the center. They alleged Amazon's morning meetings and traffic jams at the building entrance made social distancing impossible. Smalls organized a walkout, and on Monday, March 30th 2020, somewhere between 15 and 50 (depending who you ask) workers walked off the job to protest Amazon's lack of Coronavirus protections.

That afternoon, Smalls was fired. According to Amazon, Smalls was under orders to quarantine because he had close contact with a coworker who later tested positive. Amazon's official line was that Smalls was fired because he returned to the property during the quarantine period.

Later that week, leaked internal meeting notes revealed plans for an Amazon-led smear campaign against Smalls. During a meeting attended by Jeff Bezos, Amazon general counsel David Zapolsky dismissed Smalls, who is Black, with dog-whistle racist terms, saying, "He's not smart, or articulate, and to the extent the press wants to focus on us versus him, we will be in a much stronger PR position [attacking Smalls] than simply explaining for the umpteenth time how we're trying to protect workers."[23] Just to be clear: the general counsel for the world's richest company, in a room full of rich white executives including the wealthiest man in the world, thought it was a smart use of time to attack a single hourly-paid Black employee. Zapolsky kept going: "Make him the most interesting part of the story, and if possible make him the face of the entire union/organizing movement."[24] Here, before our very eyes, is Amazon creating a scapegoat, attacking a whistleblower, and creating a top-down plan to punish workers who organize to advocate for better working conditions. An employee who raised legitimate safety concerns, instead of being heard, is proposed as a punching bag for Amazon's PR strategy.

While they discussed scapegoating Christian Smalls, Amazon was also quietly capitulating to his demands. It's a common Amazon strategy for a PR crisis—refuse to admit fault, deflect blame onto a scapegoat, then quietly implement changes to address the conditions that caused the bad PR in the first place. On April 2, 2020, *The Verge* reported that Amazon workers would receive surgical masks to wear on the job to protect against the Coronavirus.[25] In addition, they'd be tested for fevers on the way into work, and anyone who had a temperature over 100.4 would be sent home. These are both important protections against the spread of Covid-19, and they came to Amazon much too late and only after Amazon tried to silence the most prominent voice calling for these protections. It's yet another example of Amazon doing something close to the right thing only after tremendous PR pressure; in this and many other cases, whatever moral compass Amazon has spins only when bad PR hovers near. Still, many say it's not enough, and that fulfillment center working conditions during the pandemic are still dangerous. Walkouts continued. Christian Smalls's platform grew. Cases spiked at many fulfillment centers. Amazon messaging about the safety of their warehouses in the midst of the pandemic was unclear and misleading. May 1 saw a general strike at Amazon facilities across the country. But little seemed to change about Amazon's willingness to protect its employees, and Amazon fulfillment centers remained risky places to work throughout the pandemic.

On top of all that, Amazon's plan to scapegoat Christian Smalls appears to have backfired. Amazon thought making Smalls "the face of the entire union/organizing movement" was a way to get rid of him and his concerns. Smalls, however, eagerly accepted the "face of the entire union/organizing movement" role, in the process starting a revolution at Amazon. More on that in the next chapter.

•　　　•　　　•

The COVID-19 pandemic was a tremendous strain on every business. Yes, even Amazon, who stood poised to increase its profits as more people shopped online. Amazon quickly abandoned its promise of next-day shipping for Prime subscribers, bumping shipments and orders of "non-essential" goods to weeks or even months in the future. What "essential" meant was, of course, not communicated transparently to Amazon's community.

The pandemic was especially hard on restaurants. For me, the entire lead-up to the pandemic was filled with moments that seemed poignant in retrospect. I had one of them on a Saturday morning in mid-March, 2020 at Ladybird Diner, a comfy modern diner run by my friend Meg. It's right across the street from The Raven's old location. Meg has always been community-driven—she has books by local authors set out on the counter. She lets local politicians use the dining room for free campaign events. I was eating brunch at Ladybird with my wife and son on a Saturday morning. The pandemic was looming. The restaurant was busy. Very busy. Homemade bottles of hand sanitizer sat on every table. Meg and I spoke briefly, when she had moments between bustling tasks. She was concerned about how busy the restaurant was. I was concerned about the author event we had the previous week that had packed 450 people into a poorly ventilated auditorium. In a few days, the governor would shut down dine-in service at all restaurants. I didn't know it at the time, but that morning at the Ladybird was my last meal at a restaurant for more than a year.

The Raven adapted—we already had strong online sales, so the pivot to a carryout/delivery model wasn't as hard for us as it was for others. Weirdly, Amazon's vague decision to prioritize "essential" things left a bit of market space for independent bookstores to carve out. Unlike Amazon, we didn't profit-gouge the pandemic, but the chance to ship books faster than Amazon for once gave The Raven a bit of security in ensuring we'd be around after the pandemic was over.

But Ladybird's tiny kitchen had long prevented it from doing any carryout at all, and now its cramped cooking space prevented any social distancing between employees. Meg was facing a cataclysm for her business. It looked like it could be worse than the time a grease fire shut her down for months right after she first opened.

Meg's reaction to this crisis was to figure out how to do as much community good as she could in these difficult circumstances. She did not bemoan the fate of restaurants, she did not solicit pity, she did not mope or shake her fist at the heavens. Facing the who-knows-how-long closure of her business, Meg quickly implemented a free box-lunch program where she and a few of her staff donned masks and gloves to prepare hundreds of free meals. Every day from 11-12, racks of hundreds of white bags were wheeled onto the Ladybird patio, free for anyone who needed them. And with the virus's economic toll spreading, a lot of people needed them.

While Amazon profited off a pandemic and hired notorious spies to monitor its workers, Meg gave up on the idea of profit at all, choosing community service instead. While Meg fed people in need, Amazon tried to go full steam ahead without any safety measures, only adapting important worker protection measures after racist scapegoating of the employee most vocally calling for them. There's only one Amazon, and it has shown its true colors. But there are millions of small businesses, and many of them found ways to keep their workers safe while still serving their communities in a time of crisis.

The epilogue to this story is perhaps my favorite illustration of the importance of small businesses to their community. After months of distributing hundreds of free lunches with no decrease in demand, Meg was looking around for ways to keep funding her efforts. One day in August 2020, Meg called me with an idea. A hallmark of Ladybird Diner's social media is Meg's thoughtful mini-essays, gorgeous little glimpses at diner life. Meg definitely has writing chops. On the phone that day, she told me she was thinking of collecting her online writing into a book, and selling the book through the Raven and Ladybird to raise money for the free-lunch program. To say I was enthusiastic about the idea would be an understatement. Meg quickly compiled a manuscript, hired a local artist to do a cover, then teamed up with the University Press of Kansas (another vital small business) to get it printed. By October 2020, the book was flying off our shelves. Sometime in 2021 it became the Raven's bestselling book of all time, surpassing its spiritual predecessor *The Paradise Cafe Cookbook*, which I'll discuss in a later chapter. From its publication date until the day in Summer 2021 that Ladybird reopened for diner service, every copy of *Ladybird, Collected* funded four free lunches. (Even though Ladybird has since reopened, folks who need it can still get a free lunch there.) Even now, people are still reading Meg's book and buying it because it's just a good book, a compassionate look at community and small business life. It's been an honor to see *Ladybird, Collected* sell alongside *How to Resist Amazon and Why*; at the Raven they're on a table together, and they both regularly appear on our biweekly bestseller lists. I think the two books are in conversation in really interesting ways. Together they form a small syllabus of small-town small-business life and the way small businesses can create community. After you finish reading this book, I highly suggest you find a copy of *Ladybird, Collected*. I should warn you, though: you won't be able to find it on Amazon.

CHAPTER 2
ON AMAZON'S JOBS

*H*ere's what you need to know about working in an Amazon warehouse: it's dangerous. Amazon uses artificial intelligence to push its human employees to their limits and beyond. Those employees are seriously injured at work at a rate double the industry average. Employees are advocating and organizing for safer conditions, but Amazon is ready to spend its massive resources to bust up any unionizing attempts. Amazon workers face many risks, from grueling quotas, to a lack of breaks, to severe weather. In order to fulfill their promises of low prices and fast shipping, Amazon *relies* on these grueling working conditions. Amazon's convenience is built on the backs of overtaxed workers. And those backs are prone to injury.

Before I talk about working at Amazon, I need to talk about working at independent bookstores. There's a lot of room to criticize Amazon about how it treats its workers, but by saying that I'm not letting my own industry off the hook. Working at a bookstore is a demanding and low-paying job. The bookstore industry has a long history of expecting people to accept low pay and no benefits, simply for the love of working in books. *Because I get to work In Books*, the thinking goes, *it's okay that I'm not making much money*. I have been working very hard to dispel this notion, both at the Raven and through industry channels like my seat on the American Booksellers Association board of directors. When I published the first edition of this book, the Raven didn't offer benefits, and I only offered part-time jobs. In the original version of *How to Resist Amazon and Why*, I wrote about how every bookseller at the Raven had another job or income source. I'm proud to say that much of this is no longer true. Several Raven booksellers fully support themselves on Raven work now. Additionally, the Raven now offers a health benefit plan. We've also added three full-time manager positions. Everyone who works at the Raven makes above the Douglas County, Kansas living wage as calculated by MIT's living wage calculator. Most importantly, as of January 2022, the Raven is now an employee-owned business. While I maintain a 51% ownership stake, 7 booksellers now own the other half of the business and will share in its profits. The more I wrote about how Amazon does it wrong, the more I wanted to try to do it right at my store. It's an ongoing effort—I would never claim that working at the Raven is a *perfect* job. And I don't write about these changes to congratulate myself, but rather in the hope that others will follow. We as an industry have a long way to go towards equity, inclusion, and making sure to treat our workers with dignity and respect. My deeply-held wish is that the book industry's widespread hatred of Amazon will manifest in better jobs for our own workers.

Bookstore owners can point to so many reasons for low wages in our industry. The wholesale costs of books are proportionally higher than other kinds of goods. The cost of employee health insurance is simply astronomical and the American health system can best be described as "fucked up" (truly the single thing that would best fix the bookstore industry is Medicare for All). Independent bookstores represent a shrinking 6-8% of all book sales, leaving a smaller piece of the pie to share with our employees. In the face of all this, perhaps it makes sense that bookstore people love to talk about how the job is about "more than money." If nobody's going to get rich, focus on the non-money perks like meeting authors or drowning in free advance reader copies, right? These things motivate me, sure, but I speak from a point of privilege. As much as I wish you could, you can't pay a medical bill with a pile of advance reader copies.

Compare all this to Amazon's October 2018 announcement that all Amazon employees would start at $15 an hour, still higher than the starting wage at many bookstores.[26] Or compare it to the ads I see all the time claiming that Amazon starts full benefits on day one. In a very basic sense, one could say that if you're interested in making more money, it's better to work at Amazon than an independent bookstore. But it's a bit more complicated than it seems.

As it stands in the United States, it's incredibly difficult for any low-wage worker to make ends meet, and that includes the bookstore industry. That also includes Amazon. But I think Amazon is deserving of special scrutiny for a few reasons. Chief among them is this: even if a new worker at Amazon starts at $15 an hour, Jeff Bezos makes $8,560,000 an hour.[27] There are many, many people not making much money at Amazon, and they are making the few people at the top of Amazon very rich. Few bookstore workers are making much money, but at least the same can be said for many bookstore owners too (Big-5 publishing executives, now that's another story). Many bookstore owners don't draw salary at all, especially in their first two or three years. For transparency's sake, my Raven salary is $36,500 a year. Jeff Bezos makes that much money in 14 seconds.[28]

Amazon is worth $1 trillion, and their former CEO and founder is by some accounts the world's wealthiest man. The fact that a company is producing tremendous wealth should automatically invite scrutiny of how that company treats its workers—what is going on at the bottom to feed so much wealth to the top? The entirety of the low-wage economy needs to be examined, and the whole country should be soul-searching about why we're so comfortable asking people to work so hard for wages and benefits that can't pay their bills. But I think a good place to start asking those questions is with the company that's making more money than anyone else.

People love Amazon—it's "the most trusted and well-liked tech brand."[29] One of Amazon's most popular initiatives is its Prime subscription, which now boasts more than 140 million subscribers.[30] A key feature of Prime is free next-day shipping on millions of eligible products. That's a lot of goods moving very quickly, and Amazon relies on a network of more than 100 fulfillment centers with 150,000 full-time employees to make fast and free shipping happen. Those employees make Amazon's most popular service possible. Those employees face grueling conditions, backbreaking demands, and a high likelihood of being injured on the job.

Journalist Emily Guendelsberger embedded at an Amazon fulfillment center for an entire holiday season for her invaluable book *On the Clock: What Low-Wage Work Did To Me And How It Drives America Insane*. In *On The Clock*, Guendelsberger outlines the relentless days of the Amazon picker: a scanner gun uses GPS technology to whip its human bearer back and forth across the gigantic warehouse to retrieve items to be packed into boxes. The scanner knows when you've stopped moving, and it tries to keep its bearer moving at the maximum possible productivity. This ruthless software-aided employee management, aimed at maximum efficiency, is spreading throughout many corners of the low-wage work world, but nobody's perfected it like Amazon's fulfillment centers. In fact, Amazon's scanners are set *above* the average worker's ability. One picker Guendelsberger talked to claimed that "rates were often set unrealistically high, which forced them to spend entire ten- and eleven-hour shifts in the weeds."[31] Another picker said, "only one or two employees a day, out of forty, makes rate," and another worker added, "anyone not getting the numbers they want to see, they get rid of them."[32] A result of the intense tempo is constant pain, so much so that Amazon places pain medication vending machines on the floors of the warehouses,[33] and repetitive stress injuries are common.[34]

Guendelsberger's time embedded in the Amazon's SDF8 warehouse is a valuable insight into Amazon's skewed sense of worker safety and health. Of particular concern to Guendelsberger is the omnipresent vending machines dispensing over-the-counter painkillers. In *On The Clock*, she writes:

Q: Your warehouse workers work 11.5-hour shifts. In order to make rate, a significant number of them need to take over-the-counter painkillers multiple times per shift, which means regular backups at the medical office. Do you:

A. Scale back the rate—clearly, workers are at their physical limits

B. Make shifts shorter

C. Increase the number or duration of breaks

D. Increase staffing at the nurse's office

E. Install vending machines to dispense painkillers more efficiently[35]

Guendelsberger continues, "what kind of fucking sociopath goes with E?"[36] The vending machines, while technically representing an innovative solution to a worker problem, also represent a way of thinking devoid of human empathy. Guendelsberger writes, "After just one week at SDF8, it's so obvious how 'hire ambulances to wait around so workers with heatstroke can get to the hospital faster' seemed like a clever, innovative solution to someone."[37] Another example of Amazon's skewed thinking was revealed in September 2018 when researchers uncovered a patent that Amazon had filed for a worker safety device: a human-sized wire cage mounted on top of a robot.[38] Amazon claims it has never implemented the cages, and it doesn't plan to. But someone at Amazon spent the time making the design and filing for a patent. That's not something you just do for fun. Even if the cages never make an appearance, Amazon thought their invention and patenting was a worthwhile investment. If it doesn't represent an actual in-use device, it still represents how the company thinks of its workers.

Despite all this, Emily Guendelsberger's conclusion after embedding at SDF8 seems to be that working in an Amazon warehouse isn't particularly exceptional compared to other warehouse work. In fact, it might even be better. Describing her efforts to interview former Amazon workers online, she writes, "Everyone said Amazon was strict bordering on obsessive about safety—'it was actually pretty annoying'—and that Amazon paid significantly better than less safe warehouse jobs in the area."[39] Amazon's own website claims that "Median pay inside our fulfillment centers is, on average, 30 percent higher than employees' pay in traditional retail stores."[40] At the end of *On The Clock's* chapter on Amazon, Guendelsberger herself tells a coworker, " . . . the impression that I got was that it was going to be hell on earth. And I didn't find it to be that way. Everyone was much nicer than I expected. It hurt way more than I'd expected, but it wasn't, like, a *hellhole*."[41] Two parts of Guendelsberger's conclusion foreshadow what would happen in the years after her time at SDF8: worker solidarity would become hugely important, and Amazon would make decisions ultimately leading to their warehouses in fact becoming hellholes.

An explosive study released in November 2019, six months after *On The Clock's* publication, dispenses any idea that Amazon fulfillment work isn't that bad. The study, a collaboration between *The*

Atlantic and the *Reveal from the Center for Investigative Reporting*, calls Amazon fulfillment centers "injury mills."[42] After acquiring internal injury records from 23 of Amazon's 110 fulfillment centers, the study finds that, "the rate of serious injuries for those facilities was more than double the national average for the warehousing industry."[43] Some individual fulfillment centers, in fact, were operating with an injury rate *quadruple* the national average. While some Amazon workers who spoke with Emily Guendelsberger for *On The Clock* seemed to think that Amazon warehouse work was in fact more safety-obsessed than other warehouse work, the *Atlantic* study clearly proves otherwise. An Amazon worker is more than twice as likely to be injured on the job as their peers in other companies' warehouses.

A February 2020 article in *The Guardian* supports the assertion that Amazon warehouse work is especially dangerous by speaking to employees of an Amazon fulfillment center on Long Island. In November 2019, during the middle of holiday peak, 600 employees signed a petition that:

> called on Amazon to consolidate workers' two 15-minute breaks into a 30-minute one. Workers say it can take up to 15 minutes just to walk to and from the warehouse break room. Workers also called for Amazon to provide more reliable public transit services to the warehouse. They also called attention to reports of high injury rates at the facility there, which were found to be three times the national average for warehouses, based on the company's injury reports to the Occupational Safety and Health Administration (OSHA).[44]

According to one of the Long Island employees, "the only changes Amazon implemented after the high injury report was published was to install video monitors around the warehouse that tell workers safety is the company's number one priority." Another employee says, "I would rather go back to a state correctional facility and work for 18 cents an hour than do that job."[45]

A 2020 book by antitrust expert David Dayen, *Monopolized,* lays out a litany of ways "The experience for workers inside Amazon's empire is, shall we say, unhealthy:"

> Algorithms determine just how many workers are needed each day, creating a labor force of nervous temps . . . Seven employee lawsuits allege that workers were fired for the crime of being pregnant. In 2018 the National Council for Occupational Safety and Health named Amazon one of America's most unsafe employers. The daily monotony and burdens to perform push workers to despair and even death.[46]

In fact, it's not unheard of for Amazon's working conditions to cause death in some cases. Labor writer Kim Kelly spoke with workers at Amazon's Bessemer, Alabama fulfillment center, who told her that six of their coworkers died in 2021, including one who had a stroke on the job after his request to go home sick was denied.[47] But even if a worker calls in sick for a legally-protected reason, Amazon still may punish them under their strict attendance policy. A 2022 letter to Amazon from Bernie Sanders and Elizabeth Warren demands an answer to reports that Amazon has punished workers for calling off for federally protected reasons like disability and family leave.[48]

If you ask Amazon to go on the record about the injuries in their warehouses, you'll likely hear about their focus on safety or the millions they're spending on trying to make their warehouses better places to work. But Amazon's public statements simply do not match the true story about what's happening in its warehouses. If you ask Amazon, increasing automation and use of robots means less worker injuries. Amazon exec Jeff Wilke told *Frontline* that robots "make the job safer."[49] By this point, we should be skeptical about any Amazon statement, and for good reason. After obtaining company records and internal documents, *Reveal* found that, in fact, "company officials have profoundly misled the public and lawmakers about its record on worker safety." So despite Wilke's PBS pronouncements, Amazon documents reveal that "For each of the past four years, injury rates have been significantly higher at Amazon's robotic warehouses than at its traditional sites."[50] Amazon's own data contradicts the story that Wilke was telling on national TV. But it doesn't stop there. If you ask Amazon, the blistering peaks of Prime Day and Black Friday don't lead to any more injuries than normal: an Amazon statement to *Business Insider* declares, "we know for a fact that recordable incidents do not increase during peak."[51] The first reason to be skeptical of this claim is that even on normal days, Amazon warehouses have double the injury rate of industry peers. Therefore, a non-increase still means abnormally high injuries. Further, documents from *Reveal* "reveal a mounting injury crisis at Amazon warehouses, one that is especially acute [. . .] during Prime week and the holiday peak—and one that Amazon has gone to great lengths to conceal." Indeed, the weeks of Prime Day and Black Friday "had the highest rate of serious injuries for all of 2019."[52] So not only is Amazon injuring workers at staggering rates, but it's also working very hard to conceal those injuries. To be clear, when I say "conceal" I mean lie. But Amazon's goal is to make the process from the buy-now button to the box on the porch as invisible and convenient as possible. My guess is that being honest about the danger of their warehouses might complicate that process, at least for customers who value workers' rights.

Questions about Amazon's warehouse safety and transparency record reached a boiling point after perhaps the biggest tragedy in Amazon warehouse history. On the evening of December 10, 2022, a line of severe storms crossed the Midwest. That night, an EF-3 tornado touched down in Edwardsville, IL. Defined as a "severe" tornado, this EF-3 was believed to have winds up to 155 mph. Edwardsville has a higher-than-average risk for tornadoes compared to both state and national averages. Even with that in mind, this was a pretty strong storm with a steep toll: the storm killed six people. All six victims were working at an Amazon warehouse called the DL14 delivery station.[53]

A smaller version of a fulfillment center, delivery stations are where "customer orders are prepared for last-mile delivery to customers," according to Amazon's website.[54] That means Delivery Centers are buzzing day in and out with Prime delivery vans, their drivers, and people preparing the vans' cargo loads. The tornado that ripped through Edwardsville on December 10th almost completely leveled DL14. Immediately, journalists and others began asking whether Amazon had done everything in its power to keep its workers safe during the powerful storm, especially since the warehouse deaths were the only deaths in Edwardsville that night. For instance, the gigantic warehouse only had one safe room, and none of the six workers who died were able to reach it.[55] (Other sources, like *The Nation*, claim the warehouse "had no form of emergency shelter.")[56] One of the reasons they didn't reach safety may have been the fact that "it is company procedure to continue working through severe weather alerts and tornado sirens; and it is company procedure to wait until a tornado has actually touched down before allowing workers to stop working and find shelter."[57] It's also unclear how much emergency training the workers in Edwardsville had; immediately after the tornado, workers across Amazon took to company message boards saying "they had never had a tornado or even a fire drill over the course of their careers at Amazon, dating back up to six years."[58] Though Illinois has no specific laws requiring workplace fire drills, the area's higher-than-average tornado risk should ideally lead to regular workplace safety training. Amazon's apparent lack of severe-weather training for warehouse employees is cause for alarm. One cause for the lack of safety training could be employee churn: Amazon boasts a staggering 150% turnover rate in its warehouses. It's hard to imagine every worker receiving comprehensive severe weather training when so many new people are starting every day.[59] The tornado also renewed scrutiny of Amazon's policies prohibiting warehouse employees from bringing phones onto the warehouse floor.[60] Amazon rationalizes the phone bans in the name of productivity, but an employee isolated from his coworkers a quarter mile from his phone in a windowless warehouse is dangerously unaware of outside happenings like severe weather. Ultimately, Amazon's message to its employees is clear: the show must go on, questions of worker safety be damned. One of the six Amazon workers killed on December 10, Larry Virden, texted his girlfriend Cherie Jones that night: "Well I will be home after the storm." "What you mean," she replied. He answered, "Amazon won't let us leave." It was the last thing he said to her.[61]

When the Edwardsville Police department held a press conference on December 11, not a single Amazon executive or official was there. Dave Clark, Amazon's head of Worldwide Consumer, tweeted vague "thoughts and prayers," neglecting to even mention the deaths.[62] On December 11, the only post on Jeff Bezos's social media accounts was a selfie celebrating an imminent star-studded voyage of his Blue Origin spacecraft. Amazon executives' hands-off response to the unfolding scope of the disaster mirrors how company policy views the people driving Amazon vans: the van drivers, and many of the people killed on December 10th, weren't actual Amazon employees; rather, they were third-party contractors. According to *The New York Times*,

> The more than 250,000 drivers like Mr. Harris who fuel Amazon's delivery network do not work directly for the company but instead are employed by over 3,000 contractor companies. On Saturday, Mike Fillback, the police chief in Edwardsville, said the authorities had "challenges" in knowing "how many people we actually had at that facility at the time because it's not a set staff."[63]

This third-party loophole is a common way for Amazon to evade responsibility. Larry Virden, for instance, may not have been an employee of Amazon but rather an employee of a small company whose only contracts are for Amazon deliveries. Even in reports of his death, it's unclear what exactly his employment arrangement was. What is clear is who was in charge: "Amazon won't let us leave." Even if Virden worked for a third-party delivery contractor, his perception was that Amazon was calling the shots, and that Amazon was the entity prohibiting him from leaving his route. Though the third-party contractors are technically independent, Amazon maintains a remarkable amount of control over them via contracts and surveillance; more on this control in chapter 3.

In terms of how prepared workers feel for severe weather, nothing has changed: according to *The Nation*, "warehouse workers say there are no new safety protocols to ensure that this tragedy doesn't happen again."[64] The Edwardsville tornado represents the most tragic possible consequences of a notorious Amazon loophole: Amazon can escape all kinds of liability about their van drivers and countless other Amazon workers, because the workers aren't employees. They're contractors. The difference may seem small but it's a huge part of why Amazon can get away with everything it does. Even more alarming is the fact that, throughout all this tragedy, Amazon didn't actually break any laws. In the months following the Edwardsville tornado, OSHA issued a "hazard alert letter" but stopped short of declaring any violations or issuing any citations.[65] Amazon may have left its employees in unnecessary danger, but it didn't break any laws, which perhaps says more about the laws than anything else.

Permanent, full-time Amazon warehouse employees face enough danger as it is, but Amazon uses a third-party loophole to wiggle out of even more worker protections for temporary warehouse workers and delivery drivers. Amazon claims a starting wage of $15 an hour for all Amazon employees. Fair enough. But the people you see driving vans full of Prime packages aren't necessarily Amazon employees. According to David Dayen,

> Thousands of delivery drivers wear Amazon uniforms, use Amazon equipment, work out of Amazon facilities, and are called by their employers "the face of Amazon.com," but are not classified as Amazon employees. That means they don't qualify for the guaranteed $15-an-hour minimum wage Bezos announced in 2018 to much fanfare."[66]

The key difference here is that the people driving Amazon's last-mile delivery vans are employed by small companies that contract with Amazon for delivery. As discussed later, some of these companies exist solely to deliver Amazon packages, but because the companies aren't *technically* owned by Amazon, the owners of these third-party companies can get away with paying their workers much less than $15 an hour. Amazon can still say that "all Amazon employees" start at $15 an hour, despite the fact that people wearing Amazon vests delivering Amazon boxes from Amazon vans perhaps aren't making that much. Amazon can also talk about offering 'Amazon employees' bathroom and lunch breaks that the third-party drivers don't get. In Spring 2021, Amazon denied reports that its third-party drivers regularly urinate in bottles during their routes in order to keep up with Amazon's crushing rate.[67] Later document leaks made it clear that Amazon was in fact aware of the peeing-in-bottles issue. Some third-party delivery companies even made employees sign a document saying they could be fired for peeing in bottles in their vans.[68] Amazon has been known to maintain tight controls over these third-party companies, even at times providing scripts for owners to use with employees. It's possible, then, that Amazon provided the language for these documents. Even if Amazon didn't provide the language for the documents, they did create the conditions that lead to the problem in the first place: even though these are technically independent third-party companies, "Amazon controls delivery drivers' routes, package quotas, and the terms of their employment, and Amazon plays a direct role in leaving drivers with few options other than to pee in bottles."[69] They can do all this and still claim that Amazon jobs are good, because of the third-party loophole. A 2019 *Buzzfeed* article asserts that:

> Amazon denies any responsibility for the conditions in which drivers work, but it has continued to contract with at least a dozen companies that have been repeatedly sued or cited by regulators for alleged labor violations, including failing to pay overtime, denying workers breaks, discrimination, sexual harassment, and other forms of employee mistreatment.[70]

Despite what their shirts say, many Amazon drivers are not Amazon employees, so take Amazon's promises of high pay and benefits with a grain of salt.

In fact, even at fulfillment centers, not all the pickers and stowers are Amazon employees. On average, a third of the workers at fulfillment centers are temps, and that percentage increases during the peak holiday season.[71] The temps do the same work at the same insane speeds, but they're not Amazon employees. Again, Amazon can make promises about benefits and high wages for Amazon employees, but it still relies on thousands of non-Amazon employees to do its work. The non-Amazon employees don't fall under the promised benefits. This reliance on third parties as a way to evade responsibility is a theme that comes up again and again when investigating how Amazon does business.

Much of what is sold on Amazon.com comes from third-party vendors, but Amazon purposefully makes it difficult to distinguish between sold-from-Amazon and sold-from-third-party items. Still, the ultimate result is that third-party vendors are contributing to Amazon's record profits and lining Jeff Bezos's deep pockets. Like the third-party truck drivers, third-party merchants don't fall under Amazon's promised $15 an hour wages. Third party sellers are not Amazon employees but they contribute to the massive riches of Amazon.

Amazon's treatment of the third-party sellers has been called strict and oppressive. David Dayen writes that Amazon's marketplace is so large that "anyone with aspirations of selling online has no choice but to sign up for [Amazon's] marketplace and abide by its rules."[72] Amazon's marketplace is so big and powerful, in fact, that Amazon essentially makes its own laws: "Amazon has disconnected this virtual mall from the normal regulatory and judicial structures, operating as its own private court of appeals."[73] It is not a fair court and it's totally isolated from federal and state laws protecting business owners. In fact, to be an Amazon seller you have to sign "the largest employment-based arbitration agreement in America, consigning millions of small businesses to Amazon's private law."[74] Dayen tells a compelling story of Amazon's overreach in regulating marketplace sellers: two sellers meet through Amazon and fall in love. They decide to move in together. When Amazon notices their stores operating off the same IP address, it blocks both accounts. The couple has to get permission from Amazon to continue their relationship. But if you ask Amazon, they're not even Amazon employees. There are thousands of people who create wealth for Amazon wearing Amazon's clothes while being told they aren't

Amazon employees. These workers are only Amazon's problem until they're a problem.

The simplest solution for labor issues like Amazon's is for the company to do the right thing and treat their workers with respect and dignity, paying them a fair living wage. If you ask me, when a company has unsafe workplaces and dangerous worker quotas, the company should simply strengthen workplace safety measures and lower the quotas. But it's hard to imagine Amazon ever deciding to fix things on their own. Amazon Prime one-day shipping is one of Amazon's most popular features, and it's the root cause of the workplace safety issues. Amazon's convenience is built on the (injured) backs of warehouse workers. If Amazon's worker issues are going to be solved, alternative solutions need to be found, one of which is collective action and worker organizing. Since the first edition of this book, union activity at Amazon (and at major corporations across the country) has skyrocketed. Facing the rise in worker organizing, Amazon has resorted to calculated, expensive, and elaborate union-busting measures.

For much of its history, Amazon staved off unionizing attempts. The first union election in company history was in 2014, when 30 maintenance workers in Delaware voted against forming a union.[75] Other unionizing efforts were stalled before reaching the election stage, in large part because of Amazon's anti-union tactics, including anti-union training videos. But Amazon's tactics went beyond the usual distribution of anti-union material: in late 2020, leaked internal documents revealed that Amazon is so determined to quash worker organizing that it hired spies to monitor warehouses and activists. According to a dramatic *Motherboard* report, "Amazon analysts closely monitor the labor and union-organizing activity of their workers throughout Europe, as well as environmentalist and social justice groups on Facebook and Instagram. [. . .] Amazon has hired Pinkerton operatives—from the notorious spy agency known for its union-busting activities—to gather intelligence on warehouse workers."[76] Sometimes, "in order to track protests and other labor organizing activity, Amazon intelligence agents create social media accounts without photos and track the online activity of workers leading organizing efforts."[77] *Motherboard* journalist Lauren Kaori Gurley claims, rightfully, that

> Amazon's approach of dealing with its own workforce, labor unions, and social and environmental movements as a threat has grave implications for its workers' privacy and ability to join labor unions and collectively bargain—and not only in Europe. It should also be concerning to both customers and workers in the United States and Canada, and around the world as the company expands into Turkey, Australia, Mexico, Brazil, and India.[78]

Hiring the Pinkerton agency, which gained a violent anti-labor reputation at the turn of the 20th century, is a clear indication of just how much Amazon opposes its employees advocating for better treatment, pay, and working conditions.

Despite Amazon's best efforts, however, a resurgent labor movement has emerged and Amazon is one of its prime targets. In March 2020, Amazon opened a fulfillment center in Bessemer, Alabama. Within months, the warehouse's workers began organizing with the Retail, Wholesale, and Department Store Union (RWDSU).[79] As soon as the workers began organizing, Amazon went into full union-busting mode. They papered the warehouse, from entrance to bathroom, with anti-union propaganda.[80] They held captive-audience meetings to intimidate workers and make threatening predictions about what would happen if a union vote succeeded, from the loss of benefits to the closure of the warehouse.[81] Sometimes multiple meetings happened in a single week, and Amazon kept track of who attended.[82] They hired cops to keep organizers away from the warehouse, an especially intimidating move since the vast majority of Bessemer workers are Black and summer 2020 saw the police murder of George Floyd and racial uprisings across the country.[83] Amazon hired anti-union consultants to the tune of $10,000 a day.[84] Amazon also retaliated against employees involved in the organization efforts, at times firing them, even though U.S. labor law prohibits firing because of union activity.[85] Amazon even asked county officials in Bessemer to change the traffic light pattern outside the warehouse, giving organizers less time to communicate with workers.[86] All told, the number of complaints about anti-union practices filed against Amazon has tripled since February 2020.[87] For the first time in its history, Amazon faced a credible union threat with its Bessemer, Alabama warehouse, and Amazon responded by literally tripling down in its malicious union-busting tactics, many of which might have been outside the scope of U.S. labor law.

Two union-busting tactics by Amazon were especially cunning. First, the union decided on an initial bargaining unit of 1,500 full-time warehouse employees. In December 2020, Amazon instead pushed for all 5,800 warehouse workers to be in the bargaining unit, adding thousands of part-time workers and third-party delivery drivers, none of whom had any contact with union organizers, therefore leaving them particularly susceptible to Amazon's anti-union propaganda.[88] Second, after the NLRB began the official by-mail union vote in February 2021, Amazon had the USPS install a "secure mailbox" in the fulfillment center's parking lot, directly in front of an entrance to the warehouse. It then texted workers, encouraging them to use their parking-lot mailbox to drop off their vote-by-mail union ballots.[89] The mailbox raised alarms. The union vote was designed to be secret, with workers permitted to vote and turn in their ballots off-site, safe from Amazon's surveillance. Remember, this is a company that hired Pinkertons to quash union activity, and here they are doing everything they can to create an unofficially official ballot drop-off onsite, in range of their cops and security cameras. Some workers even saw Amazon security guards opening the mailbox, even though it's an official USPS drop box they shouldn't have access to.[90] The RWDSU's president went as far as to call the whole mailbox ordeal "pretty disgusting."[91] There's evidence that discussions about installing the mailbox went as high as Dave Clark at Amazon, and Jacqueline Krage Strako, the USPS's commerce and business solutions chief.[92] Amazon really, really wanted employees to turn in their ballots in the Bessemer warehouse's parking lot, presumably because it could watch them do it.

Ultimately, in large part because Amazon diluted the voting unit, the vote failed in March 2021, with 738 workers voting for and

1,798 voting against. It would appear that Amazon successfully squashed its biggest union threat yet. There's good news, though. Bessemer's union drive was a key event sparking a nationwide resurgence in union activity, which ultimately led to the first unions at Starbucks stores and organizing at many other companies. And the Bessemer story isn't over; in April 2021, the RWDSU filed a complaint with the National Labor Relations Board (NLRB) alleging unfair labor practices, including the placing of the USPS mailbox.[93] In August 2021, the NLRB ruled that Amazon's conduct made a "free and fair election . . . impossible."[94] Central to the NLRB's findings was "Amazon's unilateral decision to cause the United States Postal Service to install a generic unlabeled mail collection box less than 50 feet from the main entrance to its facility, at a location suggested by the employer and immediately beneath the visible surveillance cameras mounted on the employer's main entrance."[95] In November 2021, the NLRB ordered a re-vote to occur in February 2022. As I send this book to print, Amazon appears to have won a much-closer second election with 875 for and 993 against; the elections therefore went from 29% yes/71% no to 47% yes/53% no. However, the 416 contested ballots from the second election could potentially change the results, meaning a long process of litigating those contested ballots awaits.[96] Even if the ultimate result is a union loss, Bessemer represents progress in the story of labor at Amazon. In the face of a historically brutal union-busting campaign, the union managed to increase its vote count in the re-vote, in the process bringing the issue of labor at Amazon to national prominence as part of a nationwide reinvigoration of the American labor movement.

While RWDSU was fighting traffic lights and union consultants to organize the Bessemer warehouse, Christian Smalls got busy in Staten Island. Smalls is a former Amazon warehouse worker who was fired and smeared for leading a small walkout in March 2020. The walkout was small enough, in fact, that more executives were involved in Amazon's panicked response than there were workers at the actual protest.[97] Smalls responded by starting a revolution. Together with Derrick Palmer, a friend he met while working at Staten Island's JFK8 warehouse, Smalls founded the independent Amazon Labor Union and set his sights on organizing his former warehouse. While the RWDSU ran a traditional from-the-outside union campaign, Smalls and Palmer engaged in a deeply unconventional grassroots attempt to unionize Amazon. For one thing, the ALU lacked the resources and coffers of a traditional established union like RWDSU. The ALU's entire campaign was funded by $120,000 raised on Gofundme; for comparison, in 2021 Amazon spent $4.2 million on anti-union consultants alone, just one part of their union-busting campaign.[98] Smalls' and Palmer's efforts were scrappy; they spent a lot of time literally camped out next to the JFK8 bus stop, where they made TikToks, built fires to keep departing workers warm, and posted signs that promised "free weed and food."[99] They distributed fliers about huge executive pay raises and Jeff Bezos's under-construction yacht that was so big, a historic Dutch bridge would have to be dismantled before it could get to sea.[100] Despite the humble campaign, Amazon was as determined as always to squash the effort. At one point in February 2022, Amazon actually called the NYPD and had Smalls and two SDF8 workers arrested after they brought a free lunch for warehouse employees.[101] Calling the cops! On a Black organizer! For giving away pasta! This is one of the trickiest ways Amazon and other corporations can union-bust: Amazon can require attendance at hours-long anti-union meetings, but the second an organizer wants to provide a different point of view (or, god forbid, a free lunch), Amazon can literally have them arrested. At another point, Amazon put cameras and a fence around the bus stop, limiting the number of people Smalls and Palmer could talk to. At another point, the NYC MTA moved the bus stop and locked the nearby bathroom, a move that echoes the changing traffic lights in Bessemer, where public infrastructure becomes ensnared in Amazon's union-busting.[102] Regardless, the dogged Smalls was determined to collect enough signatures for an NLRB election. Stringing together 36-hour days, phone banks, and months of superhuman effort, Smalls gathered the signatures and an election was set for early 2022.

Small's scrappy, herculean effort paid off. In late March, 2022, the Amazon Labor Union won its election with a decisive 2,654 - 2,131 vote tally (55% yes, 45% no). On the steps of the NLRB office where the vote count took place, Christian Smalls took a jab at Bezos's infamous quip about Amazon workers paying for Blue Origin by saying, "We want to thank Jeff Bezos for going to space, because while he was up there, we were signing workers up."[103] Many consider the ALU vote the most significant labor victory in a generation. A lot of people, myself included, truly wondered if a union would ever take hold at Amazon, given Amazon's massive resources and relentless commitment to union-busting. But the ALU's victory has already inspired organizing at several other Amazon workplaces; in the short weeks since the ALU's win, "Hundreds of workers from the Southwest, East Coast, and Midwest have contacted Amazon Labor Union for help organizing unions, and organized groups of warehouse workers inspired by Amazon Labor Union's victory, formed or expanded at Amazon warehouses across the country."[104] Amazon is perhaps poised to repeat what's happening at another corporate titan, Starbucks, where 20 stores have successfully voted to unionize with the Workers United union, with 200 more filing for elections. So far, only one of 21 Starbucks union votes have failed, and many of the yes votes have been unanimous.[105] It's too early to tell how much of a trend these union efforts are, and it's important to note that union success at Starbucks might not foreshadow union success at Amazon. After all, Amazon fulfillment centers are exponentially bigger than Starbucks stores, with thousands of employees vs. the dozens at a Starbucks.[106] Additionally, Amazon warehouses have 150% turnover rate, and when they're at work workers are much more isolated from each other for long stretches of time. Finally, unlike Workers United, the Amazon Labor Union is a startup union with limited resources and fewer ties to established organized labor. Such conditions notoriously make unionizing difficult. Regardless, it's certainly interesting to see an independent union like ALU succeeding where bigger, more traditional unions have failed. When discussing independent unions like the ALU, one worker at Amazon warehouse JFK8 says, "I think it's going to shake up the labor movement and flip the orthodoxy on its head."[107] Whatever the future holds, one thing is clear: Amazon's effort to silence Christian Smalls backfired in a spectacular way: after spearheading the first-ever successful union vote in Amazon history, Smalls tweeted, "Amazon wanted to make me the face of the whole unionizing efforts against them. Welp there you go!"

Smalls, Palmer, and the entire ALU (not to mention the thousands of workers who voted "yes") have a historic achievement on their hands. But there's a long road ahead, as Amazon appears poised to get even more intense in their union-busting. For one thing, they can challenge the JFK8 vote result, drawing out the process and delaying contract negotiations. For another, in the weeks after the union vote count, some new union-busting tactics have come to light. Amazon has converted some of their $10,000-a-day union consultants to full-time "blue badge" employees so they'd be able to blend in more easily.[108] One of those new blue-badge employees is far-right union buster Rebecca Smith, author of a book called *Union Hypocrisy*. Amazon hired Smith at LDJ5, a Staten Island warehouse adjacent to JFK8, while it awaited its own ALU vote.[109] Amazon really appears to be willing to do anything to stop the union; in April 2022, reporter Ken Klippenstein discovered that a new intra-company chat app bans phrases including, "I hate," "Union," "Compensation," "Pay Raise," "This is concerning," "Petition," "Grievance," "Injustice," "Diversity," "Vaccine," "Living Wage," "Representation," "Unfair," "Unite/unity," "Slave," "Freedom," "Restrooms," "Coalition," and "Ethics."[110] A company trying to ban their employees from even saying the words "freedom" or "ethics." You can't make this stuff up. As silly as it seems, it's all part of an expensive and coordinated union busting effort that remains powerful, even in the wake of the historic JFK8 victory. Mere weeks after that union win, the ALU handily lost an election at the nearby LDJ5 warehouse thanks in no small part to Amazon's anti-union efforts.[111] After their victory, Amazon began firing people involved with the union effort.[112]

Amazon promises higher starting wages. Higher than many bookstores can pay, in fact. Still, it's worth noting that working for Amazon can be a dangerous, and at rare times deadly, endeavor. Warehouse workers are pushed to make rates no humans can sustainably maintain. Delivery drivers and temp workers are considered contractors and stripped of benefits and protections. Workers are injured much more often than staffers at other companies' warehouses.

At times, these working conditions can lead to death. But these working conditions are necessary to maintain Amazon's promises of convenience and customer obsession. Whenever workers act collectively to improve their workplace, Amazon will act swiftly and with great force to eliminate organizing efforts. Before you tell Alexa to buy toilet paper, think about what's required of the humans that'll make your Charmin arrive by tomorrow.

INTERLUDE 3
ON WHETHER AMAZON AFFECTS MY WORK AT THE RAVEN

One of the ways Amazon affects my work at The Raven is how frequently people ask me if Amazon affects my work at The Raven.

In short, yes.

Has there ever been a company that looms over anything like Amazon looms over small retailers today? Is it fair that one single company casts a shadow over every record store, clothing store, bookstore, stationery store, shoe store?

The Everything Store is always on the mind of the anything store.

Sometimes we hold packages from UPS for neighboring businesses. At our original location, we didn't have a back room. So occasionally customers could walk into this outspokenly anti-Amazon bookstore and see Amazon boxes sitting on the floor. We didn't love it but we don't want to be bad neighbors.

Sometimes the Amazon Prime van parks outside our window and we joke about it. We'd never actually slash its tires because we feel solidarity with Amazon's overworked contractors, but it's cathartic to joke.

Built into our business philosophy is the idea that every single thing we sell is available cheaper elsewhere. Amazon's predatory pricing is at the root of nearly every decision we make. It's that hard to overcome that it's where we start when we think about how to do business.

You can see it when customers try not to flinch at the after-tax price of the new $32.50 Eric Larson hardcover or the $38 *1619 Project* book, available on Amazon right now for $22.50.

The first Google result for any book is the Amazon page. Amazon's inventory is more comprehensive than our distributor's, believe it or not. So you'll often see an Amazon tab open on one of the store computers for when we need to find a quick ISBN or something.

I don't mind, really, I don't, when customers show me an Amazon page when they're looking for a book. I'm not offended or that huffy that I don't want people opening *that website* in *my store*. My point is that it's so ubiquitous as to be the only place to look up information about a book. It's just one company that sells books. Publishers, the people who *put out the books*, aren't considered the default places to find information about a book. One vendor has somehow captured that distinction, despite there being thousands of places that sell books.

A customer calls. Asks about a book. We find information for them. Price, synopsis, pub date, whatever. The conversation rolls to the point where it either turns into a sale or not. "Is it in stock?" The customer asks. "No, but we're happy to order it for you and it'll be here in a few days." Often the customer answers with one of these replies:

- "Let me think about it"
- "Let me call a few other places."
- "I'll call you back"
- "I want to order it but not right now."
- "I don't want to be a bother, no, really"

Every single one of the above responses means "I'll buy it from Amazon as soon as we hang up, but thank you for doing free labor for me."

There's a lot to keep track of when running a small business. It's not always possible to immediately order toner when I get the printer's 20% warning. We somehow managed to buy a printer whose ink cartridges aren't stocked by our office supply company or any of the brick and mortar businesses in Lawrence. I haven't bought anything from Amazon in nearly four years. It gets hard sometimes. It seems like nobody ever has the ink cartridges that fit The Raven's printer. But I persevere through the streaky last gasps of the cartridge until a new one arrives from somewhere else.

I haven't ordered anything from Amazon in the last four years but the last time I did buy something was perhaps my most embarrassing bookselling story. I'll tell it to you here if you promise not to tell anyone. I'd keep it secret but it represents an important step in my own anti-Amazon evolution, seeing as it was so awful that I decided then and there to cancel my Amazon account. Not just Prime. The whole shebang. My son was a few months old and not sleeping for any significant stretches of time. I was running on patched-together 45-minute naps alternating with hourlong chunks of trying to rock him to sleep. This state of mind made me forget things. It was in this fog I agreed to sell books at an offsite event and forgot to write the event in my planner. Two days before the event, my stomach bottomed out when I got a reminder email asking if I needed anything. Yes, I silently replied. I need to order these goddamn books and no publisher or distributor is going to get them to me in less than 48 hours. I ordered them on Amazon and paid enough for shipping that I would absolutely lose money on the event, even if I did sell out. I don't even remember what I told my employees; maybe I just told them the truth. They very gracefully refrained from the ridicule I deserved when the boxes arrived. I hastily put them into some empty Penguin Random House boxes from the recycle pile and put them in my car, ready to drive off to the event.

During the COVID-19 pandemic, we were running an online event on Crowdcast with a panel of YA authors. Several of their author friends, some of significant renown, were in the digital crowd. One of the panelists mentioned a forthcoming book. One of the famous author friends dropped a preorder link in the chat. A link to Amazon. I scrambled to make a Raven link to post in the chat, hoping people would click on that one. Okay, and a little bit to make a point, though honestly this author was too famous for me to be picking fights with them. Nobody in the chat mentioned it, though later someone mentioned on Twitter that they could see my onscreen visage tense up when the Amazon link appeared.

It's not that bookstore owners are obsessive about this, though the above anecdote might make it seem so. It's just that shadow thing. We have to fight really hard to carve out a small slice of market from this behemoth of a company. Forgive us for being a bit sensitive and noticing these things.

These things like when an author retweets or shows support for our anti-Amazon advocacy, but their Twitter bio links to the book's Amazon page.

It's just that every thought we have about the business has at least a sprinkling of Amazon on it. When a customer says "I'm glad you're here," or "I'm happy to spend money here," the silent second half of the sentence is always, "in spite of Amazon."

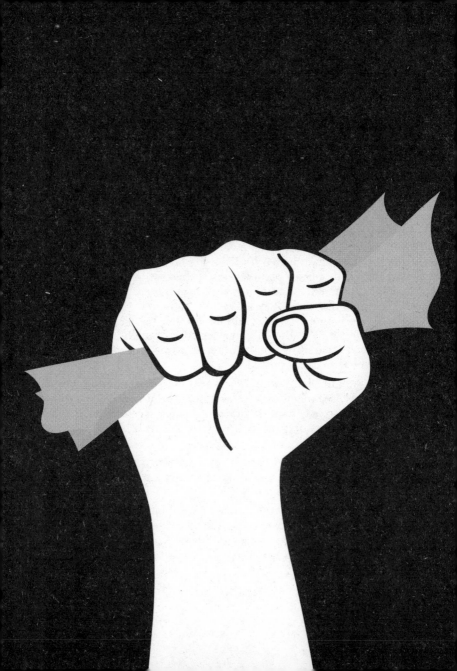

Chapter 3: ON AMAZON'S FULLFILLMENT PIPELINE

I've said it before: I'd love to be able to compete with Amazon. This book didn't come from my reluctance to compete with Amazon; it came from my inability to. The business that represents the single biggest threat to my business is a business I can't compete with because they're bending the rules of free market capitalism into something fundamentally unfair. If it continues to grow unchecked, there will be no more businesses like mine. The main trick Amazon's retail arm uses to ensure this unfairness is the act of being a platform and a user of that platform at the same time. I'll explain.

Amazon's retail arm basically has two ways of selling you things: from Amazon, and from third-party sellers.

For the first option, you give Amazon your credit card information and your address and one of its fulfillment centers sends you the item you ordered.

For the second option, you give Amazon your credit card information and your address, and after it takes a cut of the money, it sends your shipping information and the rest of your money to a person who's running a small business fulfilling this kind of order. That person sends you the item. Or, in many cases, the small business pays Amazon even more fees to let an Amazon fulfillment center ship the item for the small business.

Like anything with Amazon, it's all a bit more confusing (often on purpose), but that's the basic gist: something you buy from Amazon is either Amazon fulfilled or third-party fulfilled. Amazon is both a store and a platform on which independent sellers compete with each other. Here's the problem: Amazon is not only the host of the marketplace platform, but it's also a competitor on that very platform. And Amazon makes the rules. This means Amazon's marketplace is inherently unfair, because one of the competitors on the platform can also change the platform's rules at a blink, and everyone else has to adapt. Amazon can (and does) use its dual role as platform and competitor to skew its platform unfairly towards it.

So why don't these online sellers simply go somewhere else? Well, Amazon is an e-commerce monopoly. That means, effectively, that there *is* nowhere else. In a *Wall Street Journal* article from 2015, an aggrieved merchant says, "You can't really be a high-volume seller online without being on Amazon, but sellers are very aware of the fact that Amazon is also their primary competition."[113] That article is seven years old, and I assure you the problem has only gotten worse.

An ideal fair market system of competition would have a set of third-party enforcers, like the refs at a basketball game. Ideally, this is a pretty good thing for a government to do. Continuing the basketball metaphor: the way Amazon does things, basketball inventor James Naismith is coaching one of the two teams, acting as ref, *and* inventing new rules to benefit his own team in the middle of the game. The other team can't change the rules at all, and is in fact forced to scramble to adapt to the new rules as they come up. How can the team playing Naismith possibly win? Alternately, Amazon is the Harlem Globetrotters and Amazon Marketplace third-party sellers are the Washington Generals: one's success is built upon the idea of running all over the other. It's literally impossible for one of the teams to win at this game.

One way Amazon exploits its position as platform host and platform competitor is to steal ideas from third-party sellers to develop new Amazon-branded products. A stunning April 2020 *Wall Street Journal* investigation found just that: "Amazon employees have used data about independent sellers on the company's platform to develop competing products."[114] The *Wall Street Journal* investigation called it a "pattern;" Amazon used its role as platform manager to access data that would help it in its role as platform competitor. Amazon denies it all but the investigation was serious enough to get Jeff Bezos an alarming letter from the House Judiciary Committee, which we'll revisit in chapter 7. The letter wasn't the first time these platform/competitor practices landed Amazon under government scrutiny; in 2018 the European Union launched an antitrust investigation to determine "whether Amazon is gaining a competitive advantage from data it gathers on every transaction and from every merchant on its platform."[115] Amazon's exploitation of this competitor/platform third-party loophole gives it extraordinary power over the people who rely on its platform for their livelihoods. Amazon uses its dual roles as platform and competitor to fuel its seemingly unstoppable growth and influence.

Now Amazon is playing this unfairly stacked game with the largest and most trustworthy shipping networks in the world. As Rana Foroohar writes,

> Amazon has started a new business offering logistics and delivery services to the very retailers who are now being charged higher prices by UPS and FedEx as a result of Amazon. Merchants who sign up, most of whom are already competing with Amazon itself for sales, now find themselves at even less of a competitive advantage, thus further strengthening Amazon in the process.[116]

Foroohar here explains that Amazon is taking its platform/competitor dual role into the shipping realm, as well. Offering its own in-house shipping gives Amazon one more way to squeeze customers and third-party sellers alike. But Amazon's foray into shipping doesn't just affect sellers and customers; Amazon has basically challenged the global shipping network to a high-stakes rigged game. As Foroohar writes, "Amazon is like the House in a Vegas casino—it always wins."[117] You'd think that Amazon's tremendous volume of shipments would help the United States Postal Service and other shipping companies. Think again.

Amazon was once seen as a lifesaver for the "floundering" United States Postal Service. In his 2016 book *Neither Snow Nor Rain: A History of the United States Postal Service*, Devin Leonard describes the relationship between Amazon and the USPS as initially promising. With Amazon in mind, the USPS negotiated a new union contract permitting Sunday delivery of Amazon packages. Leonard quotes

USPS supervisor Jesse Garrett as saying, "All of a sudden, we became the premiere package delivery company, in large part, due to our partnership with Amazon and our willingness to go for seven days. Every day, you hear, 'Thank God for Amazon.'"[118] Still, years before Amazon's shipping ambitions were public, some showed valid concern about what Amazon wanted to do to the world of shipping logistics. Leonard mulls that Amazon's "loyalty in the long term is dubious," and he quotes a postal worker's union official as saying "Amazon will drop us in a heartbeat if they find a better way."[119] In his 2021 book *First Class: The US Postal Service, Democracy, and the Corporate Threat*, Christopher W. Shaw writes, "As the Postal Service's largest commercial customer, Amazon has extended significant revenues to the agency while also placing significant strain on its infrastructure and workforce. The massive corporation is busily constructing its own delivery system, however, and emerging as a competitor to UPS and FedEx, making its future use of the postal network unclear."[120]

Further muddling the story is the fact that Amazon's sweetheart deal with the USPS makes it harder for everyone else to use the vital government agency. A 2022 white paper by economists Hal Singer and Ted Tatos was the clearest-yet case for how exactly Amazon is bending the USPS near to the point of breaking. The first way Amazon bullies the USPS is making it more expensive for literally everyone else. Singer and Tatos conclude that "original empirical evidence suggests that Amazon's lucrative negotiated service agreement with the USPS has prompted the latter to attempt to recover any losses on the Amazon deal by raising prices to other customers." Because Amazon is so big and gets such a good deal from the USPS, it forces the USPS to raise prices on everyone else. Secondly, Amazon is an undue burden on the USPS because it forces the USPS to deliver only the routes Amazon doesn't want to deliver to itself. When doing so is cheap, Amazon completes last-mile deliveries with their own third-party vans. When it's too expensive, Amazon forces the USPS to take care of it. Singer and Tatos find that "Amazon has established a network of distribution facilities in primarily urban locations, leaving USPS to serve the high-cost, largely rural areas—a "cream-skimming" strategy that exploits the Postal Service's universal service mandate." Once seen as a postal savior, Amazon has now become a threat to the sustainability of the USPS. On top of that, it certainly seems like Amazon might be trying to altogether replace or eliminate the post office. In the *Yale Law Journal*, Lina M. Khan claims, "Former employees say Amazon's long-term goal is to circumvent UPS and FedEx altogether."[121]

Even if it's cheaper and faster, Amazon's vision for a replacement shipping network circumvents good jobs and union labor to create something less safe and almost entirely unregulated. Amazon's most visible weapon in its campaign to replace the global shipping network isn't barges or trains or their infamous concept delivery drones: it's the Ford Sprinter van. Sometimes they have the Prime smile, sometimes they don't. They may be beat up or double parked or swerving, but you can't deny that they're everywhere in American cities, at all hours every day. These vans are the building blocks in Amazon's ground-up attempt to build its own private, unregulated shipping network.

Amazon's strategy is this: to speed delivery and better control their logistics, Amazon is creating its own framework for last-mile delivery. Instead of entrusting an established, regulated, and unionized company like the USPS to get packages all the way to the door, Amazon will rely on existing shipping networks only to get packages to distribution centers. From those distribution centers, Amazon's own drivers will take the packages to their final destinations: the last mile. Except these drivers aren't really Amazon's own drivers: they're employees of third-party companies that Amazon contracts with. Many of them are companies built, with Amazon's help and financing, to exclusively deliver Amazon packages. Amazon then dictates everything about how these companies do business, since they're responsible for the only business the companies do. This often makes it hard to succeed: according to *Motherboard,* "Amazon's ability to change the rules on a whim, and place the vast majority of the liability for their operations on the delivery service partners, made it impossible to survive or make money as a business."[122] The most dramatic example of this are examples when Amazon has simply shut down third-party delivery businesses in as little time as two weeks, without any warning.[123] This has definitely happened, but it's hard to say how often it occurs because part of the whole deal is Amazon offering the shut-down business owners $10,000 to sign an NDA. Still, enough people have talked about it to reveal that Amazon controls every part of these allegedly "independent" small businesses, from the founding to the operations to the shut-down, to the point that the shuttered owners have to follow an Amazon-provided script when informing their employees of the closure.[124] These seemingly random shut-downs can leave owners with hundreds of thousands of dollars in debt; the heavily-used vans are pricey to maintain, for instance, or Amazon's grueling conditions lead to huge worker's comp expenses.[125] These expenses don't go away, even if Amazon pulls the rug out from the company by quickly canceling their contract. Ultimately, the third-party delivery system, which Amazon claims helps small businesses, actually harms them: according to Motherboard's Lauren Kaori Gurley, "Amazon's small business owners around the country are experiencing widespread financial distress."

So Amazon's third-party loophole allows them to defray any financial liability from last-mile delivery onto third-party small business owners. The loophole also allows them to escape liability from disasters that might happen within this loose and loosely-regulated network. In a bombshell Buzzfeed report, Caroline O'Donovan and Ken Bensinger write:

> That means when things go wrong, as they often do under the intense pressure created by Amazon's punishing targets— when workers are abused or underpaid, when overstretched delivery companies fall into bankruptcy, or when innocent people are killed or maimed by errant drivers—the system allows Amazon to wash its hands of any responsibility.[126]

These drivers are delivering Amazon packages, often wearing Amazon shirts and hats, and sometimes from Amazon-branded vans. But they're not Amazon employees, and Amazon can easily wash its hands of the dangerous consequences of the ridiculous expectations it has on speed and productivity—at times "less than two minutes per package" over an entire eight-hour shift.[127]

O' Donovan and Bensinger's report is essential reading on Amazon's shipping practices. From its very first sentence ("Valdimar Gray was delivering packages for Amazon at the height of the pre-Christmas rush when his three-ton van barreled into an 84-year-old grandmother, crushing her diaphragm, shattering several ribs, and fracturing her skull"), the Buzzfeed report makes it clear: Amazon's private shipping network is so unregulated as to be unsafe.[128] The report is a catalog of chaos: consequences of Amazon's last-mile shipping include death (anyone from a grandmother to a 10-month-old baby to a dog), countless crashes, ignoring or avoiding crucial safety devices, vans so stuffed with packages that it's impossible to see out of the windshield, union busting tactics, lawsuits, embezzlement, and for drivers skipped meals, poorly maintained vans, whiplash-inducing turnover, staggering quotas, low pay, and being forced to urinate in bottles.[129] Amazon has contracted with companies that have myriad labor violations. Some of those companies hire people with serious driving convictions.[130] The whole system is based on chaos, and it's dangerously unsafe. But it's easy to ignore this when you need a smiling box on your porch by tomorrow.

Ultimately, one thing drives my biggest concerns with Amazon's shipping: in April 2019, Amazon introduced free next-day shipping for Prime customers. The shipping practices required to fulfill next-day shipping for more than 140 million Prime customers are chaotic and sometimes violent. Pause and think about it for a second: you can buy something online at a steeply discounted price and it shows up at your door *tomorrow*. It was unimaginable for almost all of human history. But now it's a reality so convenient and enticing that many people choose to ignore what exactly it takes to make it happen. Just the last leg of that smiling box's journey has dire consequences.

Amazon evades responsibility in nearly every way—even the vans. According to the *Buzzfeed* report,

Even though the Sprinter-style vans Amazon requires its delivery providers to use weigh several times more than most passenger cars, they fall just under the weight limit that would subject them and their drivers to Department of Transportation oversight, unlike most FedEx and UPS trucks.[131]

Before you read this as innovation, consider this: Amazon has on purpose built a network of overtired, overworked drivers operating huge vans that are *just* small enough to evade the kind of inspection and maintenance required of most other delivery trucks. Amazon imposes "dizzying" quotas for daily deliveries onto the people operating these vans.[132] The drivers of these large vans don't undergo the training that operators of other delivery vans do. On top of all this, Amazon's primary concern with repairs is making sure a high brand image, so they don't require repairs on non-visible issues.[133] And what happens if something goes wrong? Amazon can wash its hands of the consequences because these are third-party companies.

In a bit of big-tech irony, Amazon is desperate to wash its hands of accountability when it comes to its drivers, but it's also desperate to keep them under close surveillance. More than half of those Ford Sprinter vans are now equipped with AI Cameras made by tech startup firm Netradyne.[134] The cameras not only see the drivers, they also monitor driver biometric data whenever they detect an "event" like distracted driving or following too close.[135] Whenever an "event" is detected, driver footage and data is uploaded so Amazon and the third-party contractor company can both see it, presumably to punish the drivers by withholding bonuses or even firing them. Drivers even get a weekly score from the cameras. Amazon says the cameras are for worker safety, but drivers themselves say the cameras are faulty and an undue hassle, even making their job *less safe*. One driver told *Vice*,

> The Netradyne cameras that Amazon installed in our vans have been nothing but a nightmare [. . .] They watch every move we make. I have been 'dinged' for following too close when someone cuts me off. If I look into my mirrors to make sure I am safe to change lanes, it dings me for distraction because my face is turned to look into my mirror. I personally did not feel any more safe with a camera watching my every move."[136]

Amazon has put these third-party drivers in a deliberate but weird position: it collects literal biometric data about their job performance, but it wants no part of the liability if something bad happens to them at work.

While Amazon makes a habit of dodging worker accountability by classifying many workers as third-party contractors, the UPS and the United States Postal Service are largely unionized, offering at least a promise of worker protection and collective bargaining power where contracted Amazon drivers have absolutely none. Further,

> Applicants for jobs at UPS and FedEx are thoroughly screened and cram for challenging entrance exams before being hired. They undergo rigorous training that can last for weeks or longer, depending on the position, and are required to undergo additional training every year. Even the most minor fender benders trigger internal investigations that seek to identify who was at fault and how such accidents can be avoided in the future.[137]

Where some may see nostalgia, I see a desire to keep delivery jobs safe and unionized, with benefits and accountability. In Amazon's shipping network, drivers sometimes go through a mere two days of training before being unleashed into environments as challenging as downtown San Francisco.[138]

Some of Amazon's packages are delivered in an even less organized manner than a fleet of private, essentially Amazon-only delivery companies. The Amazon Flex program enables people to deliver Amazon packages from their own cars. It's Uber for smiling boxes. Except competition among Amazon Flex drivers has gotten so fierce that some use special apps and even bots to attract more delivery business to themselves.[139] It's unpredictable, unsteady work, just like many big tech gig economy jobs. Many Flex drivers "have grown frustrated with the intense and often unpredictable nature of grabbing shifts."[140] One former Flex driver described Amazon's Flex business model as "tossing a fish into a bucket of lobsters [. . .] We all have to fight for a meal."[141] Amazon can safely claim that this job pays $18-25 an hour, but that's if you can even get any hours. While it might at least offer the promise of good pay, I would never call it a good job.

There are three things that concern me about how Amazon has built its private shipping network: first, its desire to usurp a shipping network that's highly regulated and largely unionized with something unsafe and unregulated. Second, I worry about Amazon's constant desire to divorce itself from the consequences of its spread and influence. Seemingly at every turn, Amazon has a way to distance itself from the effects of its dominance. Our delivery van killed your grandma? We're sorry for your loss, but it's not really *our* van. It's a third party van and the responsibility lies with this small company. Never mind that the company's sole purpose is to deliver Amazon packages or that it was founded with a loan from Amazon, it's still a *separate company*, see? What does it mean that a company is so desperate to flee responsibility? As a small business owner, I'm proud to stand for my store, its employees, its place in the community, and the merchandise it carries. Third, and perhaps most importantly, when Amazon and other big companies take distribution into their own hands, it's creating a future where small and medium-sized businesses can't compete. This was especially clear during the supply-chain disruptions of late 2021. In the face of widespread inventory and labor shortages, Amazon could easily fall back on their gigantic privatized shipping network to game the system, while small businesses fought over the dregs through the only channels available to them. As Rose Adams writes in *American Prospect*, "smaller retailers simply cannot compete with their bigger rivals in a supply chain scramble."[142] At a time when publishers now have to wait six months for a book to go to print (I'm turning in this draft on April 15th for a book that will come out in the Fall, and Microcosm tells me that's warp speed these days), Home Depot and Walmart are chartering their own cargo ships to get around goods shortages. Amazon's successful foray into the create-your-own-fulfillment-network game is sending a message to big and small businesses alike: to big businesses, it's saying, *to compete in the future you too need to take fulfillment in your own hands, USPS be damned*. To small businesses, it's saying *there's no future for a business that's not big enough to create its own private USPS competitor*.

Amazon is big enough that if it doesn't like working with anyone, it can simply create a new, more powerful, and often less safe version of whatever it's competing with. In doing so, Amazon often finds ways to evade responsibility for the fallout of its disruption. Even something as big as the global shipping network isn't immune. But I think it's important to ask: where does it stop? Will Amazon tire of working with governments to the point where it tries to supplant *them*? I'm afraid there are already signs that Amazon is getting dangerously involved with government itself. More on that in a few chapters.

INTERLUDE 4: ON THE RAVEN'S ALL-TIME BEST SELLER

*H*ere's a good story that Amazon could never tell about itself, about a book that isn't even available on Amazon.

At Harvard Book Store, the #1 bestseller of all time is *Make Way for Ducklings*. At Book Culture, if you don't count textbooks, it's *My Brilliant Friend*. At King's Co-Op in Canada, it's Kafka's *The Metamorphosis*. The Book Loft in Columbus has sold more than 10,000 copies of its all-time bestseller, *The Alchemist*. At Books Are Magic, it's Oliver Jeffer's *Hello*. At Ann Arbor's Literati, it's probably Maggie Nelson's *Bluets*, or at least it was for a while. Here at the Raven, the long-time #1 bestseller of all time was a self-published collection of recipes from a restaurant that hasn't served a plate of eggs in almost two decades: *The Paradise Café & Bakery Cookbook*.

I don't know why the Paradise Café & Bakery closed. It happened in 2003, 11 years before I arrived in Lawrence. When I wrote the first edition of this book, the storefront where the Paradise Café did business was a defunct nightclub formerly called Tonic. On the rare chance I stayed downtown late enough for Tonic to be open, I occasionally walked by a single optimistic red velvet rope with bored looking bouncers at its empty head, in front of tinted windows blinking orange and purple alongside vague bass rumbles within. Nowadays, the storefront is a very crowded bar for college students that love to flaunt public health guidelines.

I don't know why the Paradise Café & Bakery closed but headlines from the local paper arranged in chronological order tell a story that feels familiar in many of its notes:

- "Restaurants squeezed by growing competition"
- "Downtown eatery to close for remodeling"
- "Food No Longer on Tap at Paradise; Downtown Café to Focus on Bar, Entertainment"

- "Lawrence Bands Start Rockin' The Paradise"
- "Disgruntled Diner: Letter to the Editor"
- "Workers Band Together to Save Paradise"
- "Barbeque Shop May Find Home in Paradise"
- "Owner Seeks to Sell Paradise."

Though I never had a plate of Hobo Eggs and never saw the famous Hawaiian shirts adorning the walls, I feel an attachment to The Paradise Café because I shepherd hundreds of its cookbooks out the Raven's door every year.

Siblings Steve and Missy McCoy started the Paradise Café & Bakery in 1984. In 2011, eight years after the restaurant closed, Missy self-published a glossy, colorful book called *The Paradise Café & Bakery Cookbook*. It featured pictures of the Hawaiian shirts, photos of people wearing Paradise Café tees in far-off locales, and all the classic recipes from the restaurant's heyday. There are several different front cover colors, and the plastic spirals binding them together also come in a variety of colors. I'm pretty sure we're the only store in the world that sells the book. Maybe the Merc Co-op has it sometimes, too. But between the Raven's dusty walls, Michelle Obama has sold a quarter of the books Missy McCoy has sold. It's a bestseller that could only be a bestseller at the Raven.

The Paradise Café and Bakery Cookbook is not available on Amazon.

I'm not sure what Missy McCoy thinks of all this. All our interactions are business. I send her an email, she brings me a recycled paper grocery bag full of cookbooks next time she's in town. There's a handwritten invoice, and I mail a check to her country house when I get a chance. I think the first printing was really expensive. I think she has mixed feelings about the end of her time in Paradise. I think she's mainly moved on. But people keep buying that cookbook. Last time she came by she was wearing a Hawaiian shirt and I asked her if it once adorned Paradise's walls. "Oh, no," she said. "This is from Kohl's. I suppose I have a type."

I saw her in line at the bank in November 2018 and told her we were about to run out in the middle of the busy Christmas season. Did she have any more? "You took the rest last time," she said. I told her she should do a second edition, add five or six more recipes and that way people would want to buy it again. I still maintain this idea would work, but she just ended up reprinting 300 more copies of the old version. This was only after I paid for my copies upfront to help with printing costs. I pay Missy $18 for each $28.95 book, a 38% discount. This is below my normal discount, which is between 43% and 46% depending on the publisher. So I don't even make that much money on each copy of *Paradise Café Cookbook,* but I wouldn't change a goddamn thing about this book or our relationship to it. Except maybe helping put together a second edition.

I don't think Paradise Café was revolutionary. As far as I know it was just a place that served "Good, real food" in a Kansas town for a few years. Yet its memory is still a presence in Lawrence. Its archive is stories, knowing glances, a few old shirts, and one spiral-bound self-published cookbook that people keep buying. One day Chris came to work wearing a Paradise Café tee shirt that his brother had found in a closet. I took a picture of him wearing the shirt while holding up the cookbook. I posted it to our social media. Missy mentioned the post next time she was in. She mentioned that she might have some dead stock tee shirts sitting around at home. "Missy!" I cried. "We could sell those!"

"Really?" she asked.

"Yes!"

"I'll send you an email," she said with a shrug.

A few hours later I got the email: "Well, I have about 40 T-shirts—left when we closed the restaurant. They've never been sold, worn, or washed. Most of them haven't even been unfolded. I don't know if you even want to mess with them." I assured her that we did indeed want to mess with them, that they'd be perfect for our table at the upcoming town-wide sidewalk sale. She brought them by a few days later, some of them covered in cat hair. She still seemed unsure that it was even worth the hassle. Still, she drove a hard bargain. "What should we sell them for, 20 bucks?" she said.

"We try to sell our store shirts for around $15, so . . . " I replied.

"20 bucks it is," she replied.

The Sidewalk Sale is known for its early morning mobs of bargain hunters. Down the road people were banging on the locked doors at Urban Outfitters for $10 Nikes. At the Raven, I honest to goodness arrived to find a line of people waiting to buy Paradise Café T-shirts.

Short epilogue: in 2021, *Ladybird Collected,* another book about a different local diner, overtook the *Paradise Cafe Cookbook*, which now sits solidly at #2 in our all-time rankings and still sells dozens of copies every year. (Not to brag or anything, but #3 is the book you're holding right now—thanks for your support, everyone! It's an honor to be outsold by these two wonderful authors.) I think it speaks volumes about our community and customers that the three books they most want to read are all about community-oriented small businesses.

CHAPTER 4
ON AMAZON'S RELATIONSHIP TO PRIVACY AND SURVEILLANCE

*T*n the middle of the *Frontline* documentary, I couldn't believe what I was seeing. Years into my big Amazon book project, and I was still finding new ways to be shocked. The camera's angle is high, in the corner of the room. A young girl stands in the center. The room, presumably her bedroom, is full of pink and purple clothing scattered across two twin beds. A voice comes from the camera. "Come on, can you say the magic word. The girl looks up, confused. "N*****," a voice from the camera says.

"Who is that?" the girl asks, panicked.

"I'm your best friend," the camera voice vs. "I'm Santa Claus."

"Mommy!" the girl yells.

Cut to *Frontline* producer James Jacoby, asking e Limp if he had seen the video. Dave Limp, Senior Vice President Devices and Services at Amazon. Dave Limp, who invented the indoo ng camera mounted in that girl's room. The indoor Ring camera tl was easily hacked so it could spew hateful garbage at that little girl.

Limp says yes, he had indeed seen the video.

"What'd you think of it?" Jacoby asks.

Here, Dave Limp could apologize. He could say regrets Amazon's role in a child's horrifying experience. He could pi ise to do better. He's on national TV, being interviewed for a mu yped high-profile company he works for. He could take responsibility the fact that his device traumatized a little girl.

But, as is often the case with Amazon, he evades respons ity. Instead of apologizing, Dave Limp says, "I think that is an ind ry problem. It's not just about a Ring camera. It could be about anyb 's cameras."

Later in the episode, a bit of film from an Amazon meeting shows Dave Limp calling the indoor Ring camera "cute."[143]

•   •   •

Amazon is invading people's homes and privacy by employing the help of law enforcement and a fleet of technologies and systems that people are willingly buying into. In her book *Don't Be Evil*, Rana Foroohar writes "the reality of data-driven crime fighting in the United States has come to mirror dystopian science fiction," and Amazon is a driving force behind law enforcement's pivot to big data.[144] In fact, later in the *Frontline* documentary, James Jacoby quotes George Orwell's *1984* to Dave Limp directly, and Dave Limp answers, "I don't want to live in that world."[145] Reader, not only is Dave Limp living in that world. He's creating that world.

In many ways, Ring is a perfect example of the startup promise. Founded as Doorbot in 2013, it had a simple idea: app-controlled video cameras above people's doorbells to give people peace of mind about their home security. Doorbot crowdfunded a bunch of capital, went on *Shark Tank*, hired a celebrity spokesperson (Shaq, of all people), changed its name to Ring, then hit the ultimate goal: get acquired for a lot of money by a much larger tech giant. In 2018 Amazon purchased Ring for somewhere between $1.2 and $1.8 billion.[146]

Before we continue, a quick note on tech startups being sold to tech monopolies for giant sums. Big tech companies love to claim that they're innovating. But there's increasing evidence that their desire to be monopolies actually causes these companies to stifle innovation. When a company like Ring knows it can eventually sell to Amazon (or Google or Apple or Meta) for a literal billion dollars, its goal becomes making itself look as attractive as possible to these companies. That goal is not necessarily the same as creating an innovative product or doing some kind of good. The companies aren't incentivised to create the best product. They're incentivized to create what they think Amazon wants. Monopolies eliminate competition, which could eliminate innovation. Competition is healthy. A company buying all of its competitors is not. As the Institute for Local Self-Reliance's Susam Holmberg writes for

Financial Times, "in their quest to maintain dominance, tech groups are in fact killing new ideas, limiting new inventions, and blocking new businesses from getting a foothold. In short, they are undermining the vitality and resilience of the U.S. economy."[147]

Of course, it's easy to see why Amazon was interested in Ring; the two are kind of a perfect fit. On the surface, so-called "porch piracy" has become an increasing problem as people steal packages from other people's porches. Mind you, this is only a problem because Amazon has driven people away from shopping in stores and towards having things delivered to porches—it's Amazon's fault that there's more boxed booty for porch pirates to begin with. But now, Amazon was adding a valuable piece to their portfolio and a way to keep people spinning on their flywheel: are you worried about people stealing your Amazon boxes? There's an easy solution for that! Just buy an Amazon video doorbell!

But, as is often the case with Amazon, there's something bigger and more sinister going on. Through Ring, Amazon can set its sights on law enforcement and government. Amazon has launched an initiative to get police departments on board with Ring, and for police departments to get their constituents on board in turn. As of June 2020, more than 1800 police departments have signed up for programs that allow video sharing between their departments and Ring users—that's at least 10% of U.S. police forces.[148] Police can request footage from users, or users can share "suspicious" footage with police.

Ring also has aggressive tactics for getting new police departments on board. Once the police departments sign up, Ring then encourages the departments to sell Ring to their constituents with a fleet of discounts, social media strategies, and giveaways.[149] I find the idea of a company turning American police forces into sales forces deeply troubling, and The Electronic Frontier Foundation agrees. In an article called "Five Concerns About Amazon Ring's Deals With Police," EFF policy analyst Matthew Guariglia writes, "The Ring-police partnerships turn what should be our most trusted civil servants into salespeople," adding, "do police think you need a camera on your front door because your property is in danger, or are they encouraged by Amazon to try to make a sale?"[150] Additionally, Ring is putting words directly into the police's mouths: Amazon, "a large multinational corporation whose objective is to maximize profits, dictates what your local police department can and cannot say about the efficacy or necessity of Ring."[151] Through a host of materials and pre-packaged messaging, Amazon is turning police forces into Ring salespeople. Amazon Ring already makes a culture of distrust and profiling among neighbors too easy. When you add a deal that turns police into salespeople for a single corporate monopoly, it raises red flags.

Aside from all that, Ring can make life more difficult for Amazon workers. We've already been over the indignities faced by Amazon van drivers, from crushing quotas to biometric surveillance to inadequate severe weather protection to being forced to pee in bottles in their vans to working for a company that doesn't even see them as employees. Add Ring cameras to that equation: when delivering to Ring-equipped houses, Amazon drivers go from their Amazon-surveilled vans to an Amazon-surveilled house and back. They are literally never not being watched by Amazon cameras, a fact Amazon probably welcomes. Now, though, Amazon Ring cameras are helping engagement-hungry social media users add one more indignity to Amazon van driving life: Amazon drivers are being forced to dance. A TikTok trend in early 2022 goes like this: leave a note on your door telling your Amazon driver to dance. Pull the footage from your Ring camera. Post the footage on your TikTok account. Wait for folks to start clicking that little heart. Writing for *Motherboard*, Gita Jackson gets it right when she says "The implications here are horrifying on a number of levels."[151] First, because of Amazon's oft-stated customer obsession policy, the drivers are under tremendous pressure to perform or face a negative review, which can lead to losing their job (even though their job is not, in fact, to dance on camera for strangers). Even worse, if the customer puts dancing directions in the order instructions, drivers who don't dance are technically not fulfilling the order properly, raising the risk of negative reviews. One Amazon delivery company owner is quoted in *Motherboard* saying, "Technically if the delivery associate doesn't follow the instructions they can get dinged on their metrics for not doing so."[153] Another terrifying aspect of this trend is the dystopian vibes (to borrow social media parlance). Strangers are being turned into content without consent. It could even be worse than just that. Follow me on this thought experiment: Amazon van drivers are predominantly people of color. Residents of big suburban houses are predominantly white. The Amazon driver dance trend, then, often means wealthy white people hiding behind their surveillance cameras demanding that not-wealthy people of color dance for them, so they can post it to their social media accounts. It's not a stretch: that's exactly what appears to be happening in one of the most popular Amazon driver dancing videos. A post from TikTok user @itsjustleah (who appears to be white) has 6.5 million views. The video shows a Prime driver (who appears to be Black) on @itsjustleah's front porch, dancing (but not smiling). Presumably, @itsjustleah has demanded that the driver do this, without ever seeing or talking to the driver (though she, of course, can see him). It's a nightmare straight out of science fiction.

Ring is far from the most sophisticated part of Amazon's surveillance portfolio, and it's also not the most racist. In 2016, Amazon launched a cloud-based facial recognition software with a name that sounds like something *else* from a science fiction novel: Rekognition. According to Amazon's website,

> Amazon Rekognition makes it easy to add image and video analysis to your applications using proven, highly scalable, deep learning technology that requires no machine learning expertise to use. With Amazon Rekognition, you can identify objects, people, text, scenes, and activities in images and videos, as well as detect any inappropriate content. Amazon Rekognition also provides highly accurate facial analysis and facial search capabilities that you can use to detect, analyze, and compare faces for a wide variety of user verification, people counting, and public safety use cases.[154]

The ACLU claims that, "these tools don't work as pitched and threaten our privacy rights and civil liberties."[155] Despite the fact that Rekognition is widely deployed—though, given Amazon's notorious secrecy, it's hard to say exactly how widely—there are concerns that it's not quite as effective as promised. One test run by the ACLU found that Rekognition falsely identified 28 members of Congress. Instead of politicians, the software matched their faces with criminals.[156] This is concerning, of course: while there's no harm for these Congresspeople in this innocent ACLU test, the same can't be said for someone arrested and charged based on a false face recognition match. Even more alarming, though, is that the mismatched faces in the ACLU test were "disproportionately of people of color."[157] The criminal justice system already disproportionately targets people of color. If their facial recognition tools do the same, it further skews an already skewed system. Despite evidence that Rekognition is flawed, Amazon presses on, including the software as a central piece of contracts with law enforcement agencies of all kinds, including pitching it to ICE as a way to identify immigrants.[158]

The way I see it, Amazon has two methods for eroding privacy as we know it: Ring video doorbells and Rekognition facial recognition technology. I, for one, am terrified that they might end up becoming one and the same. It's scary enough that millions of homes have already plugged into an extrajudicial video surveillance network; but even more terrifying is the notion of those cameras getting upgraded to include facial recognition technology. They could then include the facial recognition data in the reports they send to police departments. The problem is, Rekognition is inaccurate with people of color, and police violence is disproportionately targeted at people of color. If Amazon equips Ring Doorbells with facial recognition technology, it's easy to imagine people of color being even more victimized by the police. And there's evidence Amazon is thinking about it: in a leaked memo from April 2020, Amazon sent a survey to Ring beta testers asking about interest in "potential new features for Ring includ[ing] [. . .] facial, and license plate detection."[159] Further, at the 2020 CES conference in Las Vegas, Dave Limp "hinted at a future in which Ring cameras could use Amazon's facial recognition technology."[160] In a post titled "Ring's Stance on Facial Recognition," Amazon writes "Ring does not use facial recognition technology in any of its devices or services." Note the definitive use of present tense; the statement gives no indication of future plans. Another hint at those future plans emerged in December 2021 when journalists uncovered patents filed by Amazon that would upgrade Ring cameras to "be able to scan neighborhoods and identify 'suspicious' people based on their skin texture, gait (walk) and voices," and also create "a 'Neighborhood Alert Mode' that would send an alert to other neighbors after a user shares a picture or video of someone found suspicious that prompts other doorbells to start recording—even if the person does not come up to their doorbell."[161] The inclusion of "skin texture" in that list is about as clear as dog whistles get. As with the robot-mounted human cages, an Amazon patent doesn't necessarily mean the nightmare idea will come to fruition. But it does mean Amazon is thinking about it enough to pay people to file the patents.

The relationship between technology, police departments, and privacy exploded into new immediacy in late Spring 2020, after Minneapolis police officer Derek Chauvin murdered George Floyd, an unarmed Black man. All of a sudden, police abolition and defunding went from fringe radical ideas to the heart of national conversations. Naturally, facial recognition technology, with its targeting of people of color and its close relationships to law enforcement, came under even more scrutiny. Even before 2020's renewed focus on how law enforcement targets communities of color, the ACLU "argued that [facial recognition] posed a particularly 'grave threat to communities, including people of color and immigrants,' in a nod to studies that have shown that facial recognition software regularly misidentifies people of color."[162] In response to Spring 2020's new discussion about how police victimize people of color, IBM permanently abandoned its facial recognition initiatives, with its CEO saying the company "firmly opposes and will not condone uses of any technology, including facial recognition technology offered by other vendors, for mass surveillance, racial profiling, [or] violations of basic human rights and freedoms."[163] Did Amazon follow suit with IBM's passionate renouncing of facial recognition? Well, they did stop letting police use their facial recognition tool. But only for a year.[164] And, in the three weeks immediately after George Floy's murder, as they kicked the facial recognition can down the road, Amazon enrolled 29 more police departments in its Ring partnership.[165] Given the chance to examine its role in the violence police perpetuate on people of color, Amazon continued to expand its dangerous program.

•   •   •

Amazon isn't reaching its tentacles into surveillance and law enforcement unopposed. In fact, much of the information in this chapter wasn't volunteered by Amazon. Rather, dogged activists and journalists uncovered it with Freedom Of Information Act requests and determined reporting. But there are signs that this kind of pressure works. Starting in 2019, UCLA began considering incorporating facial recognition software into its on-campus security cameras. Yet in early 2020 it abandoned its plan in the face of pressure from an advocacy group called Fight for the Future.[166] Part of Fight for the Future's resistance stemmed from tests it ran with Amazon's Rekognition software. Their tests found that Rekognition "incorrectly matched the faces of black people to other people's mugshots."[167] Amazon's own employees have also raised alarms about Rekognition. In June 2018, a coalition of Amazon employees wrote a letter to Jeff Bezos demanding that he pull away from ICE negotiations, writing "We refuse to build the platform that powers ICE, and we refuse to contribute to tools that violate human rights."[168] Amazon is characteristically dodgy about what exactly it does for ICE, so it's unclear whether Rekognition ended up being part of the partnership.[169]

While the UCLA and Amazon employee protests are examples of effective resistance, Amazon is still determined to secure big government contracts, and facial recognition surveillance is part of that effort. If they didn't have their eyes on the government, why else would Jeff Bezos be remodeling a lavish mansion with a huge ballroom in Washington DC?

•   •   •

While Amazon has its eyes on the government and front porches, it has ears inside millions of homes. In 2014, Amazon launched the Echo, a so-called "smart speaker" which contained Alexa, a "digital assistant" you could talk to. Alexa can play music, turn lights on and off, answer questions, and, oh yeah, buy stuff on Amazon. It's a fun trick, and it seems like an exciting vision from a Star Trek future—a talking computer! But Jeff Bezos and crew are taking it very seriously—an estimated 10% of Amazon's annual R&D budget goes to the ten thousand employees in the Alexa division.[170] Ultimately, Alexa "is designed to feel like an ever-present companion so that Prime members who use her will get sucked more deeply into the Amazon vortex."[171]

Once Alexa sucks you into the Amazon vortex, she doesn't really let go. The question of whether Alexa is "always listening" is important and largely unresolved. In *Don't Be Evil*, Rena Foroohar writes, "While reports of Alexa and Siri "listening in" on conversations and phone calls are disputed, there is no question that they can hear every word you say."[172] Many have raised questions and concerns about exactly how often Alexa is listening, and what that means.[173] Even irregularities like random bouts of Alexa laughter emitting from Echo speakers speak to how unpredictable these devices are.[174] Startlingly, one ten year-old girl asked Alexa "for a challenge to do" and Alexa said, "Plug in a phone charger about halfway into a wall outlet, then touch a penny to the exposed prongs."[175] Honestly, that makes Alexa sound like kind of a sociopath, not the kind of AI entity I'd want listening to my every word. And then there's the question of what "listening" means. Is Alexa's microphone always on? And how easy is it for some stranger in an Amazon shirt to hear the goings-on of your private home? Again, as always, Amazon is slippery on this answer. They don't say humans are listening, but they also don't say humans *aren't* listening.[176] In fact, human members of the Alexa team *do* listen to recordings "captured in Echo owners' homes and offices. The recordings are transcribed, annotated and then fed back into the software" in order to improve Alexa's AI.[177] This seems like something I'd want to know before I plug this thing in. When someone buys an Alexa, they aren't clearly warned that humans can hear what they say in their Echo's presence.

One thing is for sure: Amazon records and stores everything you ever say to Alexa, and human employees can access it. BBC reporter Leo Kelion submitted a request to Amazon for all the data it had about him. What he found was staggering: "the level of detail is, in some cases, mind-bending," he writes.[178] For one thing, Amazon had saved all 31,082 of his family's Alexa requests, including some audio clips.[179] His daughter asked for "Let it Go" 48 times—now Amazon can target ads to her. Amazon also had saved "2,670 product searches [with] more than 60 supplementary columns for each one, containing information such as what device I'd been using, how many items I subsequently clicked on, and a string of numbers that hint at my location."[180] Amazon keeps track of every click, gesture, and move a customer makes in any of its spaces and it hangs on to that data. This is central to their mission. Former Amazon executive James Thompson echoes many others when he says Amazon "happen[s] to sell products, but they are a data company."[181] And while Amazon promises they're only using data for trustworthy purposes, the sheer amount of data they collect is cause for concern. Additionally, there's evidence that they're not careful with the data—one German customer who requested his data from Amazon instead received 1,700 voice recordings of a total stranger.[182] The picture painted by the data was so clear that journalists were able to identify the stranger based on his Alexa recordings alone.[183]

Since the first edition of this book, new concerns have come to light about how careful (or not careful) Amazon is with these gigantic troves of customer data. A November 2021 report from *Reveal* finds that the Amazon division in charge of protecting customer data "in a state of turmoil: understaffed, demoralized, worn down from frequent changes in leadership and—by its own leaders' accounts—severely handicapped in its ability to do its job," leading to troves of customer data becoming "so sprawling, fragmented and promiscuously shared within the company that the security division couldn't even map all of it, much less adequately defend its borders."[184] It certainly seems like Amazon is ill-equipped to handle the sheer scale of the customer data it collects. Even worse, that data is easily accessible to an alarmingly high number of people who work at Amazon, leaving Amazon "wide open to "internal threat actors.""[185] This isn't just theoretical; according to *Reveal*,

> Across Amazon, some low-level employees were using their data privileges to snoop on the purchases of celebrities, while others were taking bribes to help shady sellers sabotage competitors' businesses, doctor Amazon's review system and sell knock-off products to unsuspecting customers. Millions of credit card numbers had sat in the wrong place on Amazon's internal network for years, with the security team unable to establish definitively whether they'd been unduly accessed. And a program that allowed sellers to extract their own metrics had become a backdoor for third-party developers to amass Amazon customer data [. . .] Amazon had thieves in its house and sensitive data streaming out beyond its walls[186]

Amazon is obsessed with collecting your data. It is not obsessed with protecting it. What emerges from Amazon's watching and listening habits is a company that's obsessed with gathering customer data. Their constant refrain is that they're obsessed with customers, but their obsession doesn't just stem from making sure customers are happy. They're obsessed with being able to hear their customers and record what their customers say in their own homes. They want to see out of their customers' front doors in high definition. According to Amazon, this is all in the name of safety and customer convenience. Amazon wants customers to trust them with their data, citing these good intentions as evidence. But it's worth bearing in mind three things we know about Amazon: data is incredibly profitable to them, they are incredibly ruthless in getting what they want, and they are less than careful once they have it. Do they want to watch you and listen to you to keep you safe, or do they want to watch you and listen to you to wring more profits out of you?

There's mounting evidence to the former, as Amazon continues to expand Alexa's capacity. At the end of July 2020, Amazon began rolling out a long-teased feature called "Hunches," where Alexa asks the user questions, instead of vice versa.[187] If Alexa doesn't have to wait for humans to activitate her to collect data about consumers, Amazon will be able to not only monetize our data much more easily, but it'll ingrain itself even more into the daily life of its consumers. Imagine how much data Amazon could know about you if you just spent all day talking to Alexa. That could be Amazon's goal, as they develop ways to put Alexa in your car and other places outside your home. It all "means the instant feedback loop, in which Amazon can roll out features, test them and receive immediate customer response data, is only growing in value for Amazon."[188] Amazon is showing no indications that it's slowing down its efforts to make money off your data, and they're never clear on the rules of that lucrative game.

Look at the foundation Amazon is laying: making sure governments at all levels are dependent on Amazon products and services. Facial recognition. A massive private video and audio surveillance network. Somewhat surprisingly, people aren't having this surveillance network forced upon them—they're opting in and *paying for it*. For now, Amazon's intentions, at least according to them, are good. But consider what happens if all these pieces combine: door cameras, facial recognition, in-house microphones. Do we trust a secretive and ruthless company like Amazon with powerful tools of this scope? As David Priest writes for *CNet,* "Perhaps, like the hours of time we spend on our phones each day, we'll arrive at a new norm without ever having time to seriously consider the route we're taking, the destination ahead. Or perhaps, the time to consider such things is now."[189]

INTERLUDE 5
ON PARTNERING WITH AUTHORS

*B*ryn Greenwood can tell you stories that'll make your hair stand on end. Bryn Greenwood has the cell phone numbers of several people who regularly don full suits of armor. *Vogue* has called Bryn Greenwood a "Hidden Cultural Gem." Bryn Greenwood is the one in long sleeved head-to-toe black in the family vacation photo. Bryn Greenwood is one of "our" authors. The relationship we share with Bryn is representative of the best author partnerships with bookstores, and Amazon has no interest in cultivating this kind of relationship.

There's no bar mitzvah ceremony when an author goes from "a local author" to "one of our authors." The process is different for each author. With Bryn, it happened like this: we did a launch party for her book *All The Ugly and Wonderful Things*, her third novel but first with a big publisher. Bryn lives in Lawrence, and we try to throw launch parties for authors who live here as much as we can. The party went pretty well: we hosted about 50 people and sold 20 or 25 books. In the months after the party, the book started selling more. People were telling each other about this thrilling, vivid story and its unforgettable characters. This word-of-mouth energy enabled Bryn to grow a big online fanbase. Fans started asking her about where to get signed copies. Presumably because we're the bookstore closest to her house, Bryn started sending people to our website. We'd let her know when orders would come in, then she'd come sign the books before we sent them off. We did a steady business in online orders of signed Bryn. At some point during all of this we became "her" bookstore, and she became one of "our" authors. I can't tell you when, but I can tell you we'd do anything for Bryn.

Writing a book is a solitary endeavor, full of long hours alone, many of them riddled with doubt. The moments when a writer emerges from the dark cave of writing, into the brightly populated world of promotion, can feel like leaving a movie theater in the middle of the afternoon. Why is the sun so bright? In Bryn's case, she started her promotion for her new novel, *The Reckless Oath We Made*, at the spring 2019 meeting of the Midwest Booksellers Association in Decorah, Iowa. It was fun for us, from a Raven perspective, to see our Midwestern bookstore friends learn what we already knew about Bryn: that she's a great speaker, a hilarious person, and her books tell stories that matter about distinctly Midwestern people. I have fond memories of the unofficial afterparty with Bryn, a bunch of MIBA folks, and basically the entire staff of Decorah's Dragonfly Books sitting down for beer and pizza at Toppling Goliath Brewing Company. The beer was great, the food was good, and the bonds between authors and booksellers thickened. Somewhere in the boozy joy Bryn told me she wanted to do a preorder campaign for *Reckless Oath* through The Raven.

Preorders are a big deal. Everybody says it, and it's true. Every preorder is added to a book's first-week sales total. If a book sells 500 copies in its first week, but it had 1,000 preorders, all of a sudden its first week total triples. The conventional wisdom goes that a book's first week is its best chance to get on the *New York Times* bestseller list. Preorder numbers are a huge factor here, as are first-week media appearances and the book tour. A book that makes it onto the *New York Times* bestseller list has a better chance of staying on the list. *NYT* bestsellers have much better sales than books that aren't on the list. For many shoppers, the *New York Times* Bestseller List is one of the biggest marks of validity a book can have.

From a much more pragmatic bookstore standpoint, there's good money in preorders. It's hard work to chip away at the perception that Amazon is the only place to place preorders, but if you can do it, it's a nice way to sell 25 or 30 or sometimes even 200 extra copies of a book. It really helps when an author like Bryn Greenwood tells their fans to preorder from you and not anywhere else. Even better is when the author offers a bonus. A month after Decorah, Bryn and I had lunch at Ladybird Diner across the street (every restaurant in this story is a great place, which is part of the reason I love this story so much). Over our cheeseburgers, Bryn told me her plan: she'd send her online fans to The Raven to preorder *The Reckless Oath We Made*. She'd then create beautiful bookmarks with custom wax seals. The only way to get a signed copy with a fancy bookmark would be to preorder it through The Raven's website. Let's see Amazon try to do that.

We sold 48 in the presale. Those aren't *New York Times* bestseller numbers. No orange "#1 Bestseller In . . . " flag will appear next to your book's title after you sell just 48 copies of anything. But you know what? Bryn's book was a #1 bestseller *here* before it even came out. *The Reckless Oath We Made* was #1 the next time we updated the bestseller shelf after its release, and that was before the release party. We hosted that, too. Because Bryn was so enthusiastic in driving sales to us, we were motivated to throw a really great party for her. There was cake. There were knights, too. That'll make sense after you read the book.

Aside from being able to partner with Bryn on a preorder campaign, another reason we were so excited about this book is that it depicts a life that lots of New York literary fiction ignores. These aren't students at a writing workshop (how many Iowa Writing Workshop stories are we going to get this year?). This isn't the slow dissolution of a family with a beach house. Bryn's books are populated with down on their luck people, sometimes making bad decisions, but always deeply realized. They're working class. They're convicts. They're hoarders. They have mental illness and chronic pain. They struggle for money. Bryn paints them sympathetically, but she doesn't give them a free pass to sainthood. Her characters still fall in love and do exciting things even though they've never been on a Subway, though perhaps they've eaten at one.

And guess what? Bryn's middle-of-the-country book is doing well at this middle-of-the-country bookstore. Maybe we should think about Kansas before we think about New York. Bryn came into the store to sign those 48 copies and I took a picture of her signing. She mentioned that, even though it was a far cry from pictures she'd seen of debut authors signing copies in shiny conference rooms on the 40th floor of Manhattan high-rises, signing that pile of books made her feel like a big shot. I told her to forget the high-rises, she was already a bestseller right here. I hope she felt seen and appreciated the way we felt seen and appreciated every time she told a faraway fan to order her book from us. In a few weeks, Bryn can come in here and see her book in the #1 spot on our bestseller shelf. Number one bestseller in *her* bookstore. We may not have a view of the lower Manhattan skyline—we don't even really have a skyline—but there's a great diner right across the street.

CHAPTER 5

ON AMAZON'S EVERYTHING STORE PROBLEM

For many years, Amazon worked hard at becoming The Everything Store. Everyone else had to grapple with the consequences of that decision; with its outsize power and influence, any decision Amazon makes sends shockwaves across the entire American economy. But now, Amazon is beginning to face Everything Store consequences of its own.

• • •

My mom was so proud: I was quoted in *The New York Times*. The article by David Streitfeld ran under the headline, "In Amazon's Bookstore, No Second Chances for the Third Reich." Streitfeld had noticed my *How To Resist Amazon and Why* zine and interviewed me for an anti-Amazon perspective. Bonus: he even mentioned the zine in the article. In the online version of the article, you can click on the title of my zine; the link takes you to the zine's Amazon page. I've often spoken about how in-article links enable Amazon's monopoly in online bookselling. Still, just for fun, I clicked on the link to my zine's Amazon page. I always enjoy the irony of seeing it up there. But this time I noticed something different: Amazon had stopped offering the zine for direct sale. Often on Amazon it can be hard to tell whether you're buying from Amazon directly or whether you're buying from a third-party seller. Generally you know you're buying direct if you see the phrase "Ships from and sold by Amazon.com." That phrase was now erased from my zine's page.

Before Streitfeld's article was published, every time I happened upon the zine's Amazon page there was always a direct buy button. Interestingly, the promised shipping speed was "usually one to two months." The reason for this, according to an email from Microcosm Publishing CEO Joe Biel, is "based on supply chain logistics." As an effort to prevent Amazon from dictating their terms of sale, Microcosm is one of the few publishers in the U.S. that doesn't sell directly to Amazon. If a Microcosm title is available as Buy Direct on Amazon, Amazon has pulled the book's data from a catch-all publishing database to create the book's page. Then, Amazon orders inventory from a place that Microcosm does sell to, like giant wholesaler Ingram. In my zine's case, Ingram was frequently backordered as *How To Resist Amazon and Why* became popular, so Amazon's fulfillment speeds were slow. But the morning Stretifelt's article appeared, somehow, Buy Direct wasn't even an option. There were only a few third-party sellers with names like "SuperBookDeals" offering mostly used copies of my zine for well above its $4.95 MSRP. At some point, Amazon decided to stop offering my zine directly. On Twitter, Streitfeld himself tweeted, "Hard to believe Amazon would pull the plug on someone's book just because I quoted him about Amazon, but also hard to come to any other conclusion here. I've reached out to Amazon for comment but so far silence." Biel wrote in an email, "it's hard to interpret it as anything but punitive." I don't know when exactly my zine's Buy Direct button disappeared. I often checked the zine's Amazon page, but I didn't check it every ten minutes and I don't have a screenshot of the exact minute the Buy Direct button disappeared. Still, that's kind of the point—neither I nor Microcosm have heard anything about Amazon's decision. According to Biel, "Amazon does not communicate whatsoever. As a publisher, you literally have to pay them to communicate with you." Even the Raven has a list of policies for how we curate our shelves. We share that information with authors who want us to stock their work. But Amazon's decisions about what goes on their shelves are much, much more consequential than the Raven's, and much harder to parse. Streitfeld's article demonstrates a huge problem with Amazon: they're trying to transition from a "we'll sell anything!" model to "we're getting rid of inappropriate or dangerous things." Amazon seems to be trying as hard as they can to undergo this transition in private. The results are a process that's vague and apparently capricious. It has disturbing free speech implications. Normally I'd say a bookstore can decide to sell and not sell whatever it wants; indeed, curation is one of bookstores' strengths. But, to me, that logic goes out the window when we're talking about a literal bookselling monopoly. Amazon is no small, curated bookstore—it's a gigantic company responsible for most of the book sales in the U.S. If Amazon is big enough to bend the trajectories of governments (more on that later), it's big enough to bend the trajectory of free speech. I know I'm paying close attention.

• • •

Even if Amazon's identity is shifting from "we'll sell anything" to "we'll try not to sell dangerous things," Amazon still definitely sees itself as both the platform and a competitor on that platform. As discussed elsewhere in this book, this platform/competitor duality creates unfair competition. It also makes it impossible for Amazon to control the items on its virtual shelves. In the past, Amazon has shown no interest in controlling what appears on those shelves, resorting to its classic third-party argument. They might even say something like "they're not *our* shelves, the shelves belong to third-party vendors." But the banner at the top of the page still says Amazon. The box it arrives in probably says "Amazon." The van and the driver's shirt probably say "Amazon." And the thing inside the box could be deadly.

A disturbing 2019 *Wall Street Journal* report sheds devastating light on Amazon's counterfeit problems. Reporters Alexandra Berzon, Shane Shifflett, and Justin Scheck found that "4,152 items for sale on Amazon.com Inc.'s site that have been declared unsafe by federal agencies, are deceptively labeled or are banned by federal regulators."[190] But this is not a question of simple bootlegs: more than 2,000 of those items pose health risks for children.[191] Amazon's refusal to police what's for sale in its marketplace can be deadly. Amazon's dedication to being the Everything Store means you could buy something on Amazon that could harm or kill you or your loved ones, and Amazon is slow and secretive in doing anything about it.

When I talk about Amazon resistance with the Raven's customers, the availability of counterfeit products is rarely the thing that gets people fired up. People deplore the fact that Amazon is putting indie bookstores out of business. People roll their eyes in dismay at how little Amazon pays in federal taxes. But nobody seems to get Real Mad about the bootlegs. I assure you, this is a highly dangerous aspect of how Amazon does business, and it terrifies me. It's not just a matter of a company trying to protect its copyrights; indeed, the availability of counterfeit merchandise on Amazon could be a matter of life and death.

The *Wall Street Journal* investigation is shocking. The *WSJ* found toys for children with lead levels that exceed federal limits. They found products for infants that failed safety tests. They found toy sets of high-powered magnets that have been banned for years because, if swallowed, they could tear through the walls of internal organs.

A man named Albert Stokes died in a motorcycle accident wearing a helmet purchased on Amazon.[192] Stokes's mother blames her son's death on Amazon, saying the helmet was listed on Amazon as DOT compliant even though it had been recalled for noncompliance. Amazon settled the eventual case for $5,000 without admitting fault. Amazon's justification? According to Amazon, *Amazon* didn't sell the helmet, it just provided a platform for the seller to list it. It's another instance of the regular pattern: Amazon uses its third-party marketplace to avoid liability for the consequences of its business decisions.

Despite its refusal to accept responsibility, Amazon quietly removed the helmet's listing, as well as hundreds of others that the *Wall Street Journal* flagged in its investigation. However, "Within two weeks of Amazon's removing or altering the first problematic listings the Journal identified, at least 130 items with the same policy violations reappeared, some sold by the same vendors previously identified by the Journal under different listings."[193] Amazon's approach to dangerous products being sold on its marketplace is a game of Whack-A-Mole. Amazon is not good at Whack-A-Mole.

Amazon is a trusted brand—one study found it the third most trustworthy entity overall, trusted more than Oprah, the police, extreme weather warnings, and teachers.[194] Naturally, this trust extends to everything you can buy through Amazon.com. But the assumption that anything on Amazon is trustworthy is incorrect and could lead to drastic consequences. During the beginning of the Coronavirus outbreak in Spring 2020, Amazon's informal web of Kindle content farms started spewing out unresearched, unedited self-published books about Covid-19. Amazon's Whack-A-Mole approach to the elimination of dangerous material once again failed to protect customers as sketchy and harmful misinformation spread across Amazon's bookstore. Mirroring their decision to remove Nazi material, Amazon quietly (and without admitting wrongdoing or providing transparency into their process) began removing Coronavirus titles. But you never really finish a game of Whack-A-Mole. Louise Matsakis, a *Wired* reporter, still found 700 mostly sketchy Coronavirus titles. She wrote, "Many of these books appear to be self-published and of low quality,"[195] with issues ranging from conspiracy theory speculation parading as fact to outright plagiarism. A cash-grab "University Press" rip-off biography of Dave Grohl is one thing. But when the same shifty approach is used to create faulty books about an extremely dangerous pandemic, the problem of Amazon's shitty self-published books becomes something else entirely. Similarly, Amazon's decision to cut back on Nazi material is eternally doomed to fail. In early 2022, *The Daily Beast* found an absolute trove of literal fascism all over Amazon's bookstore, despite a policy banning "content that we determine is hate speech" (which of course Amazon doesn't define).[196] No matter how much they try to rein in this dangerous misinformation or racist propaganda, Amazon cannot fully stop being complicit in the spread of dangerous products and information.

•　　　•　　　•

The availability of counterfeit merchandise is far from the only problem with Amazon's third-party marketplace. Because Amazon serves as both an e-commerce platform and a competitor on that platform, Amazon has an unfair advantage over every non-Amazon seller on its platform. Amazon has abused this power. A 2020 *Wall Street Journal* investigation found that Amazon "employees have used data about independent sellers on the company's platform to develop competing products," despite the fact that Amazon has long claimed "it doesn't use information it collects from the site's individual third-party sellers."[197] (If you're not going to use it, why collect it?). According to *The Wall Street Journal*, which interviewed more than twenty former Amazon employees, Amazon's private-label business used information from its third-party sellers to decide everything from "how to price an item, which features to copy or whether to enter a product segment based on its earning potential."[198] A 2021 report by *Reuters* confirms the practice, finding that not only does Amazon steal ideas and manipulate its platform to boost its own products, but also that two high-level executives signed off on the strategy.[199] All this despite the fact that Amazon has denied the practice in sworn testimony in 2019 and 2020.[200] This is a perfect example of the abuse of power enabled by Amazon's third-party marketplace system: Amazon says they provide a platform for small businesses to sell online, but there's always a threat that Amazon will steal those small businesses' ideas for their own products. A 2019 Amazon-produced document called "2019 Amazon SMB Report" claims: "Our mission is to work every day to support and champion small and medium-sized businesses." Despite promises (and lots of expensive commercials) declaring that Amazon is a friend to small businesses, the Amazon marketplace can be a vehicle for exploiting and abusing online mom-and-pop shops.

Businesses selling on Amazon's marketplace don't only face the risk of their proprietary information being stolen by Amazon; they also risk Amazon's punitive and capricious disciplinary system for third-party sellers. Amazon's marketplace bureaucracy is, by many accounts, a government in itself. According to *The Verge*, "For sellers, Amazon is a quasi-state. They rely on its infrastructure—its warehouses, shipping network, financial systems, and portal to millions of customers—and pay taxes in the form of fees. They also live in terror of its rules, which often change and are harshly enforced."[201] Amazon seller and blogger Dave Bryant has said, "sellers are more worried about a case being opened on Amazon than in actual court."[202] "Amazon is the judge, the jury, and the executioner," Bryant adds.[203] The appeals process for

Amazon's disciplinary actions against sellers is notoriously "secretive, volatile, and often terrifying."[204] The punishments are so severe, in fact, that they've become a ruthless part of competing on Amazon; since it's so difficult to come back from suspension, Marketplace sellers often sabotage other sellers in hopes of getting them suspended. One way of doing this is buying fake reviews, not for your products but for the products of your competitors. An entire mini-industry of Amazon appeal lawyers has sprung up. Amazon Marketplace is becoming an economy and government in itself; Amazon Marketplace alone is the biggest online retailer in the U.S., more than twice the size of Amazon itself.[205] The problem with a single company becoming a government in itself is that the real government can't regulate it: "It's harder for regulation to grasp a company that, rather than monopolizing a market, has become the market itself."[206] Amazon Marketplace is so big and so powerful that many companies feel like they have no choice but to endure the sabotage, unpredictability, and fear of selling on the Marketplace for fear of losing out on the sales. It's too big to avoid. Amazon's marketplace is not a platform for supporting small businesses; it's a platform for controlling and exploiting them.

One example of Amazon's whims spelling certain doom for a small business: *The American Prospect* outlines the story of Intimate Rose, a company founded to sell devices to help women recover from pelvic floor dysfunction. PFD affects as many as 1 in 3 women, and Intimate Rose makes some of the only FDA-approved over-the-counter devices to treat it. Being a small business in 2022, they're faced with the impossible choice of whether to sell on Marketplace and thus fork over huge seller fees, or forego Amazon and miss most of their market. Intimate Rose decided to sell on Amazon, but Amazon decided to categorize their FDA-approved medical devices in the "adult" category. That means these FDA-approved medical devices were right there alongside the vibrators and fleshlights. The move makes Intimate Rose's products invisible to searches and ineligible for advertising, a situation which will likely cause Intimate Rose to lose 80% of their sales. *The American Prospect* editor David Dayen writes, "With little choice but to sign up with Amazon to reach the masses, small businesses must play by, and often get burned by, Amazon's mercurial rules, and its light policing of a marketplace that can operate like the Wild West."[207]

It's hard to say the average consumer even knows whether they're buying direct from Amazon or from one of these third-party sellers. Perhaps Amazon likes it this way, and obfuscates an item's source on purpose. *Marketplace Pulse* claims, "the Amazon marketplace is also the most overlooked player in the U.S. e-commerce. Amazon doesn't mention it often, retailers and brands are focused on Amazon the retailer, and shoppers don't notice it thanks to FBA (Fulfilled by Amazon) and Prime. It's impressive how much sales volume goes through it almost invisibly."[208] Indeed, the two primary tools for this obfuscation are FBA and Prime shipping. As explained earlier, in the basic sense Amazon's system can either send you an item you order from its warehouses, or it can tell a third-party business to send you the item you order. But here's where it gets complicated: those third-party sellers can sign up for Fulfilled by Amazon, so their products are stored and shipped from Amazon warehouses. According to *The Verge,* "With Fulfillment by Amazon, all sellers have to do is ship their goods to Amazon's warehouses; Amazon handles storage and delivery and bestows a Prime checkmark on their listing, a promise of speedy free shipping and easy returns." FBA, of course, costs the businesses money, just one more way for Amazon to work its massive leverage over third-party sellers. It could also, conceivably, bury search listings from third-party sellers who don't opt in to expensive FBA or Prime upgrades.

The end result of all this is that Amazon skims a staggering amount of money off of every Marketplace sale. A significant 2020 report from the Institute for Local Self Reliance found that Amazon seller fees are increasing twice as fast as overall sales, and on average, Amazon keeps 30% of every Marketplace sale.[209] For reference, a really good year at my bookstore means a 5% profit, and many small businesses operate on similar margins. Handing over 30% of sales would make it impossible for many small businesses to survive, which undoubtedly contributes to the massive turnover in Amazon Marketplace vendors. According to the ILSR, "The vast majority of those who start selling on Amazon's site fail within a few years."[210] Further reporting by ILSR adds that Amazon's collection of third-party seller fees doubled from 2019 to 2021, making seller fees the fastest-growing revenue source at Amazon.[211] Amazon Web Services, widely perceived as Amazon's cash cow, generated $61 billion in revenue in 2021. Amazon collected *double that* in seller fees.[212] If you're wondering why Jeff Bezos can buy such a big boat, look first to the 30% his company skims off of every marketplace transaction. Many of these come in the form of Prime fulfillment, but a significant amount of seller fees come from the sale of ads on Amazon. To put it simply: Amazon Marketplace sellers have to buy ads *on Amazon* in order to compete *with Amazon*. Amazon is in fact the third-largest advertising business in the world, totaling $32 billion in revenue.[213] A huge portion of that advertising is simply people buying ads on Amazon. But here's the catch: Amazon can claim as much of this ad space as they want for free; it's their platform. As author and activist Cory Doctorow puts it, "Amazon has tied a $32b anchor around its sellers' necks, then asked them to compete with its knockoffs of their products by outbidding them in search- and product-pages, on which Amazon can top any third-party bid by writing an unlimited check to itself."[214] Advertising on Amazon has gotten so out of hand that *Marketplace Pulse* claims "everything on Amazon is an ad."[215] Amazon's product pages were originally full of recommendation algorithms and shopper-oriented suggestions. Now, however, "The last remaining recommendation functionality is 'Frequently bought together.' Everything else on the product page, including additional display advertising, is an ad."[216] Aside from drowning in ads being a deeply unpleasant shopping experience, Amazon's obsession with getting ad money from small businesses is extortion, pure and simple. It would be a lot easier to overlook Amazon's extortion of third-party sellers if those sellers had any alternative places to go, but they effectively don't. The ILSR report claims that "In 15 of 23 major product categories, the tech giant captures more than 70 percent of online transactions. Companies large and small must either sell on Amazon or forfeit access to much of the market." This impossible choice—lose access to the market or lose 30% of every transaction—is a quiet but vital way Amazon maintains its explosive growth and its chokehold on the retail marketplace.

The end result of this is Amazon Marketplace becoming more and more impossible for the small businesses it promises to help. Even if a small business can squeeze the margins enough to buy the right kind of advertising and pay for Prime status, Amazon is always there as a competitor. Amazon has stolen small businesses' ideas to make their own products. Amazon can take whatever advertising it wants for free, even though its marketplace sellers are paying literal billions for the same privilege. And now, there's a new threat for these small businesses: Amazon's Marketplace is increasingly being taken over by mini-Amazons called Aggregators, or gators for short. A gator is simply a company that buys up successful Amazon Marketplace small businesses. This idea is so attractive to tech investors that in 2021, ecommerce gators raised $12 billion in capital.[217] One of the gators, Thrasio, reached "a valuation of $1 billion within two years of its founding, making it the fastest U.S. company to ever reach what the startup world calls "unicorn" status."[218] It is now valued at $5-10 billion. Again, I stress: the only thing this company does is buy existing Amazon Marketplace sellers, and investors are throwing literal billions of dollars at it. Amazon's monopoly is so big that it's inspiring mini-monopolies within it. Cory Doctorow writes, "Gators are like miniature Amazons: markets where success is based on capital, not quality. They are systems for multiplying investor cash, not by making better products at better prices, but by outmaneuvering smaller rivals who can't afford to bribe Amazon to give them pride of place."[219] This whole gator thing is like monopoly Inception. *We heard you liked monopolies, so we put a monopoly inside your monopoly.* Thrasio "estimates that 1 in every 6 U.S. homes have purchased a Thrasio-owned product."[220]

When Amazon started gobbling up the U.S. retail market, its consolidation and predatory practices made it next-to impossible for small retail businesses to thrive. Now the same thing is happening *within* Amazon's marketplace: you have to be huge, and backed by Silicon Valley billions, to succeed. Those gators have no problem forking over their 30% and buying the right ads, because Silicon Valley venture capitalists are literally throwing billions of dollars at them. The gators can also boost their profits by copying Amazon's predatory-pricing and data-mining playbooks; more business consolidation means less competition and more customer data, after all. None of this looks good for those small businesses Amazon claims to support. According to *American Prospect*, Thrasio and other "Gators can best be understood as a euthanizer of Amazon independent sellers, providing a less painful path to their inevitable death."[221] As outlined in this chapter, the Amazon Marketplace seller faces so many indiginites, whether from a capricious judicial system or exorbitant seller fees or buying exploitative advertising. Increasingly, sellers are answering the impossible choice of whether to sell on Amazon by just selling to a gator. The gators know it; Thrasio has even published a free book called *Getting Your Ecommerce Business Ready for Sale*. Amazon is squeezing and extorting individual small businesses, and the gators are ready to gobble them up. A Thrasio employee has been quoted saying that, "having worked at Thrasio, I cannot imagine being an individual seller."[222]

Ultimately, for the consumer, everything about an Amazon Marketplace purchase, from the smiling box to the smiling van to the smiling shirt on the delivery driver, makes it seem like the product comes from Amazon. This illusion is part of the reason why Amazon Marketplace has gotten so huge: *Marketplace Pulse*'s Juozas Kaziukėnas is quoted as saying "Amazon's ability to hide the chaos of its Marketplace from consumers is part of what made the company successful early on, says. While eBay is obviously a bazaar, Amazon looks like a traditional retailer."[223] Technically, the third-party seller "gets the sale," but Amazon gets all the brand recognition and loyalty, not to mention 30% of the take, leaving the third-party seller a faceless and hidden part of a big machine. Even if a small business can figure out a way to make it in the face of these impossible terms, they face competition from Amazon itself, plus a flock of mini-Amazons gobbling up their peers with venture capital billions. It's bad for the consumer too: every product page is just a barrage of ads, and product quality is ignored in favor of market share, leading to what Cory Doctorow calls "the crapification of everything" Amazon sells.[2214] All of this as Amazon runs ad campaigns touting how much they help small businesses.

INTERLUDE 6

ON BORDERS

*A*mazon isn't the first giant price-slashing competitor The Raven has endured. The Borders Books & Music across the street from my bookstore opened in November 1997.

It wasn't without a fight. For more than a year, concerned community members fought the developer's plan, seeking to preserve both the independent-business character of downtown Lawrence and the historic character of its buildings. Original Raven owners Pat Kehde and Mary Lou Wright were central in the fight. In an homage to our region's history, it became known as "The Borders War." In the end, Borders was allowed to knock down the historic building as long as it preserved a bit of it in the new facade.

Lawrence Journal World, sometime in September 1997: "Borders bookstore's arrival to the Winter Block, just down the corner from The Raven between Seventh and Eighth streets on New Hampshire Street, is a concern for both bookstore owners. 'We have a lot of repeat customers and have gotten to know them well,' Kehde said. 'We hope the store's reputation for personal service and its unique, knowledgeable staff continues to keep them coming back to our store.'"[225]

Topeka Capitol Journal, October 1997: "Kehde believes her store's emphasis on personal service and knowledge of books will help separate Raven from the chains, even though she knows she can't always compete when it comes to price because of the larger discounts offered to the superstores by publishers and distributors. But Kehde is hoping price isn't the only thing customers care about. She is hoping quality of selection, a personal relationship with the person selling the book and having direct interaction with customers is also important—and will allow The Raven to continue to survive."[226]

It's the same argument we make about Amazon today: what we have to offer customers is more authentic, more personal, more human than what's offered by our much larger and cheaper competitor.

The headline from that 1997 *Topeka Capital Journal* article: "Small bookstores struggle as giants rewrite industry." Sound familiar?

A quote from that article: "As an independent bookstore, The Raven Book Store in downtown Lawrence is a survivor, and co-owner Pat Kehde hopes it can continue to survive. But the prognosis isn't good."

Later in the same article, again from Pat: "It's a bummer . . . I think it's inevitable that a store that big will hurt us."

The Raven's net sales in 1998 were 15% lower than they were in 1997. Sales continued to fall throughout the early aughts. We're doing better now, but adjusting for inflation, 1997's numbers were still 18% above even 2019's. We may never see 1997 levels of sales again.

The day of the Borders grand opening saw regulars descend upon The Raven en masse. As balloons waved outside Borders, The Raven broke its all-time single day sales record.

Pat Kehde, again in the *Topeka Capital Journal*, October 1997: "I think the citizens of Lawrence and everywhere else need to have the opportunity to shop at locally owned businesses and independent bookstores where all the decisions aren't made in New York, or Ann Arbor, or Dallas, or Amsterdam, for all we know," she said.

During the Borders Era our customers developed a tradition where they'd browse Borders's huge inventory, then special order what they wanted from The Raven. It's the exact inverse of what we call Showrooming today: the act of browsing a bookstore only to buy cheaper from Amazon.

Kelly has worked at The Raven since the middle of 1997. She predates (and postdates, I guess) Borders, and she's one of two current Raven employees that's worked for all the store's owners. When she started working at The Raven, she was a graduate teaching assistant at The University of Kansas and for her English 101 class, she invited Pat Kehde and the Borders manager to her class for a debate. "Really?" I said. "Did they know each other? Did they get along?" Kelly replied, "no, and no."

In 2018, original Raven owners Pat Kehde and Mary Lou Wright teamed up to write a history of The Raven for a local self-published history book. In it, they write:

> It turned out that The Raven Bookstore could survive the competition from Borders, the nearby monster bookstore chain. In 2011, after fourteen years, Borders closed their doors. We credit our success to our special attention to customers, our active connection to the community, our knowledge of the collection of books that we stocked. And, significantly, from 2005 onward, the competition from discounted online retail sales, especially Amazon.com, became lethal for the national brick-and-mortar chain stores. And The Raven lives on.

But I wonder if the same strategies that helped Pat and Mary Lou weather the Borders storm will help us survive Amazon, a much larger and more powerful company.

Kaw Valley Small Business Monthly, August 2002: "The future for small bookstores in general may be more bleak. "[Pat Kehde says,] We're in for some serious times here. A lot of small bookstores are closing. The owners are older and want to retire, and the younger people aren't opening stores."

A month after I bought the store, the Raven had its 30th anniversary. All the preceding owners took a picture with me by the cake.

CHAPTER 6

ON AMAZON AND THE ENVIRONMENT

*T*n July of 2021, Jeff Bezos retired as Amazon's CEO, leaving the reins to longtime exec Andy Jassy. In the months since stepping down as CEO, one of Bezos's preferred ways to spend his time has been taking suborbital joyrides with celebrities on his Blue Origin spacecraft. At this point, you could argue that the space flights are simply rich people having fun; they are breaking no scientific ground, despite their high cost. NASA's first suborbital flight was in 1961, and it was 5 minutes longer than the average Blue Origin flight. But no matter: Jeff still gets to put on a cowboy hat and take expensive rides into space with the likes of William Shatner while Amazon workers are crushed by brutal quotas in fulfillment centers. Bezos accidentally acknowledged this point after the first Blue Origin flight when he said, with no apparent trace of irony, "I want to thank every Amazon employee and every Amazon customer, because you paid for all of this."[227] You know who else paid for the flight? The planet. Calling these vanity suborbital flights "incredibly problematic," Physical Geography professor Eloise Marais estimates every person flying on Blue Origin boasts a carbon footprint 100 times bigger than a typical long-haul airplane flight.[228] Weird, because these climate-destroying flights are part of what Bezos thinks is the *solution* to the climate crisis. At one event, explaining his motivations for going into space, Bezos said "We will run out of energy on Earth. This is just arithmetic. It's going to happen."[229] The solution, then, is colonizing space. Apparently a 10-minute suborbital flight with William Shatner is the first step. It's striking to see Bezos's confidence in saying this, especially since the company he founded is a major contributor to the very energy crisis he feels the need to flee. This is just one of many examples of a disconnect between Amazon's words and actions on the climate crisis.

In June 2020, Amazon bought the naming rights to the diamond-shaped arena near the base of the Space Needle in Seattle, home to the new Seattle Kraken NHL team. No surprise there: expensive, high-profile naming rights deals are commonplace among huge corporations like Amazon, leading to such magnificent monikers as Cleveland's Rocket Mortgage Field House and Louisville's KFC Yum! Center. Plus, it makes sense that Amazon would go after Seattle's arena; Seattle is Amazon's hometown, and arena naming rights are just another step in their continued effort to remake their hometown in their image. But the Seattle Kraken would not play in the "Amazon Center;" rather, their new home would be called Climate Pledge Arena. Inspired by Amazon's 2019 climate pledge, the naming rights deal was a clever piece of branding to make people (try to) forget about some of Amazon's environmental misdeeds. *No matter what you've heard*, the presumed corporate logic goes, *here's a Green company putting their Green branding on a Green arena*. According to the press release dutifully recycled by major news organizations, the Climate Pledge Arena would

> build on the Climate Pledge's focus on sustainability and carbon neutrality. Amazon said it will be the first net zero carbon certified arena in the world, generate zero waste from operations and events and will be powered with 100% renewable electricity. It will also use reclaimed rainwater in the ice system to 'create the greenest ice in the NHL.[230]

Jeff Bezos himself chimed in to say, ""Instead of naming it after Amazon, we're calling it Climate Pledge Arena as a regular reminder of the importance of fighting climate change."[231] Unfortunately, if Amazon were truly committed to fighting climate change, then they'd be fighting against themselves. When it comes to the environment and the climate, the combined effect of Amazon is less Climate Pledge and more Kraken. Amazon's massive delivery footprint is a polluting strain on the atmosphere, they lie about their environmental impact, their empire of facilities perpetuates environmental racism, and their corporate actions actively silence employees who try to speak out.

As of 2016, the USA's biggest source of carbon dioxide emissions isn't, in fact, smoke-belching coal power plants. It's not the power industry at all. It's transportation.[232] When we think of emissions, we should no longer think of scary smokestacks on the outskirts of town. We should think of the Amazon vans on our own street.

Transportation-derived emissions began trending upward around 2013, and it's no mystery what one of the driving forces is (excuse the pun). Only a quarter of transportation emissions come from medium or heavy-duty trucks, the kind you see lumbering down every interstate at all hours.[233] Rather than traditional semis, a growing share of emissions comes from, you guessed it, Amazon vans: "increasingly the impact is coming in what people in the world of supply-chain logistics call "the last mile," meaning the final stretch from a distribution center to a package's destination."[234] Only one company has spent the last decade—the very decade that transportation emissions have started growing again—obsessively building a gigantic, decentralized last-mile shipping fleet: Amazon. It can't possibly be a coincidence that, as Amazon turned its attention to hyper fast last-mile shipping, transportation emissions began to rise.

It's hard to pin down the exact carbon footprint for one type of shopping versus another, for many reasons. One reason is how many variables there are. So the question of which is "greener," shopping at a store or shopping online, is a bit complicated, and the answer is basically "it depends." *Vox* claims that traditional brick and mortar shopping is largely better in terms of emissions:

> Before the online revolution, the majority of last-mile deliveries were to stores, which tended to cluster in areas that can be more easily served by large trucks. Today, most packages are now going directly to residential addresses. We've traded trips to the mall, in relatively fuel-efficient cars, for deliveries to residential neighborhoods by trucks and other vehicles. The last mile today ends on our doorsteps.[235]

According to this line of thinking, the traditional brick and mortar shopping setup is greener because bigger trucks take fewer trips to fewer spots. Since Amazon's model requires more vans going to basically every house, there's more pollution and more truck traffic in neighborhoods. On the other hand, in her book *Buy Now: How Amazon Branded Convenience and Normalized Monopoly,* Emily West argues that online shopping *could be* better for the environment. According to West, home delivery of goods overall should have a smaller environmental impact because a truck dropping off items in a neighborhood covers fewer miles than individual drivers going back and forth to a shop [. . .] Another study shows that even taking into account the carbon impacts of the additional packaging and computing required to send items to customers' doorsteps, the carbon impacts are still greater for brick-and-mortar retail, primarily due to customers' own transportation emissions.[236]

So there's a bit of calculating, and if Amazon were to do everything right, it *could* represent a greener way of doing things. What does doing everything right look like? West offers several suggestions, including using hybrid and electric delivery vehicles, deemphasizing expedited shipping, relying less on shipping by air, and providing shipping options that include transparent data about environmental impact.[237] Much of this would make business sense for Amazon, in theory, since they lose money on next-day Prime shipping. But Amazon has no interest in doing any of these things. Next-day Prime shipping is one of Amazon's most popular programs, and Amazon doesn't want people to peek behind the curtain at the environmental costs of getting their packages delivered so fast. And there are costs. Any possibility that online shopping could be greener than traditional retail goes out the window when shipping speed is a top priority; next-day shipping means more airplane flights, inefficient truck routes, and thousands of gasoline-powered vans in countless residential neighborhoods.

One of Emily West's ideas in *Buy Now* is really interesting to me, both in its possibilities and in thinking about why Amazon hasn't implemented it. West writes, "Given the environmental concerns that some consumers have about ecommerce, it's a missed opportunity not to present shipping options in terms of their estimated carbon impacts."[238] Imagine how customers could be incentivized to opt for earth-friendly shipping. I mean, in a perfect world, isn't eco-friendly shipping the free option rather than next-day? And wouldn't a little graphic saying something like "picking 5-day shipping equals planting

100 trees" make the heart-on-sleeve folks among us opt for that instead of instant gratification? Turns out, there *are* ways to find eco-friendly products on Amazon, but they're hidden: according to Yale's Anastasia O'Rourke, there's a program to "find eco-friendly and green products [on Amazon]. But you need to know about that program to even find it. So it's not necessarily something that they're putting front and center yet."[239] Amazon has even briefly flirted with the idea of letting people pick eco-friendly shipping: in *Fulfillment*, Alec MacGillis writes that Amazon "considered offering consumers a "green" option for purchasing—allowing more time for deliveries in order to reduce carbon emissions—but nixed it, fearing it might lead to fewer purchases overall."[240] And there you have it: Amazon's planet-straining next-day shipping is just too popular. Even though greener shipping would *save Amazon money*, they won't do it because their bedrock central philosophy is customer obsession, and plenty of customers are obsessed with Amazon for the simple reason that Amazon is the fastest place to buy anything online. As Emily West writes,

> If making consumption frictionless for its users is at the center of its philosophy and has helped it become the behemoth that it is, then inviting customers to reflect, on a purchase-by-purchase basis, on the infrastructures, labor, and emissions that make products appear at their door is anathema to Amazon's winning formula.[241]

But there's one more reason why Amazon won't implement some kind of green-shipping initiative, even if it makes business sense, even if they've put the words "Climate Pledge" in giant neon green on a Seattle arena: doing so would require Amazon to be transparent about their environmental impact, and they seem determined to avoid just that.

While it sounds ideal (and even money-saving) for Amazon to offer an eco-friendly shipping option, doing so would require an un-Amazon admission: that their fast shipping is bad for the planet. Amazon is really committed to being perceived as lightning-fast *and* earth-friendly *at the same time*, even if those two goals are at cross-purposes. Amazon's committed pursuit of good PR on both climate and convenience has led to a massive deception campaign that finds them lying about the true size of their carbon footprint. A 2022 *Reveal* investigation finds that Amazon "washes its hands of the climate impact of most of the things it sells" by simply deciding "to play by different rules than its peers."[242] According to *Reveal*, when a place like Target calculates its carbon footprint, it counts the emissions involved in making every single product on its shelves. Amazon, however, "takes responsibility for the full climate impact only of products with an Amazon brand label, which make up about 1% of its online sales."[243] Third-party sales take up 60% of Amazon's retail presence, and other companies' products sold by Amazon account for another 39%. Amazon doesn't consider any of that stuff as part of its carbon footprint, even though it obviously is.

We wouldn't know any of this if it were up to Amazon. What Amazon wants us to know is that they made a big climate pledge and named an expensive arena after it. But even as it publicly pledged about corporate emissions accountability, Amazon refused to join thousands of other companies in reporting to the nonprofit CDP, or Carbon Disclosure Project. Amazon's avoidance of reporting to CDP led Greenpeace to call Amazon "one of the least transparent companies in the world in terms of its environmental performance."[244] In 2021, Amazon finally submitted a report, but they asked that it not be released publicly. That didn't stop the folks at *Reveal*, so we now know that Amazon is trying to use its trusty third-party loophole to evade responsibility for its carbon footprint. While other companies reported emissions based on everything they sold, Amazon only reported emissions from the manufacture of Amazon-labeled goods like Kindles and Alexas. When Target files with the CDP, they take into account the emissions required to make every single product on their shelves. Amazon, on the other hand, replies with their trusty old third-party refrain: "they're not technically *our* shelves." Even though Marketplace sales account for the biggest slice of Amazon's revenue, Amazon has simply decided to not count any of those products or sales when calculating their carbon footprint. The end result of this creative math is the staggering claim that Amazon had lower emissions than Target, even though Amazon had four times the sales, and Target doesn't have thousands of vans spewing emissions in neighborhoods across the country. This creative emissions accounting has consequences. Amazon's big-time, much-hyped climate pledge has them promising to be carbon-neutral by 2040. That goal seems much more attainable when you're only counting emissions from 1% of the goods you sell. According to *Reveal*'s Will Evans, accurate climate accounting would make Amazon's Climate Pledge impossible:

> If Amazon were counting its footprint like some of its competition, it would have to get rid of tens of millions more tons of carbon emissions—by radically transforming its business, forcing suppliers to change their own operations, paying for enormous amounts of controversial carbon offsets or maybe even confronting whether The Climate Pledge is compatible with Amazon's business model after all.[245]

Eliza Pan, a spokesperson for Amazon Employees for Climate Justice, says "It seems like Amazon is misleading employees and the public [. . .] or even being straight-up deceptive about how well it's doing against its climate goals."[246] Even with the creative reporting to the CDP, Amazon is still not off to a great start with its Climate Pledge: Amazon's "reported carbon footprint increased just over 36% from 2018 to 2020."[247] If it seems hard to get real data on Amazon's emissions, or hard to make green choices when shopping on Amazon, that's because Amazon wants it that way. But they don't want you to look at the data. They want you to look at the big fancy sign that says "Climate Pledge."

Much like Amazon's business goes well beyond boxes and vans, Amazon's environmental impact is much broader than its retail arm and shipping network. Amazon's breakneck expansion has impacts in every city they expand to, and communities of color are disproportionately targeted. It goes without saying that an Amazon Fulfillment Center or distribution facility is a magnet for air pollution and carbon emissions; every day dozens of semis and hundreds of delivery trucks leave and return to each facility. Amazon's refusal to meaningfully invest in low- or zero-emission vehicles means that these thousands of truck trips spew tons of carbon emissions into the air. By some estimates, that "ton" is literal; one study found that the increased traffic associated with a new Amazon facility would "collectively emit 1 ton of air pollution daily."[248] But here's where it gets more complicated, and more sinister: an analysis of publicly-available data has found that 80% of Amazon's U.S. warehouses "are located in zip codes that have a higher percentage of people of color than the majority of populated zip codes in their metropolitan area."[249] Put simply, Amazon's pollution-spewing warehouses are almost always spewing pollution into communities of color. A *Consumer Reports* study backs up the finding, declaring that "Most Amazon warehouses are in neighborhoods of color," and that residents of these neighborhoods "face increased air pollution from trucks and vans, more dangerous streets for kids walking or biking, and other quality-of-life issues, such as clogged traffic and near-constant noise."[250] Further, this kind of air pollution has immediate health costs:

> Breathing in tiny particles from diesel and gasoline exhaust increases a person's chance of getting asthma, developing cancer, or having a heart attack, decades of studies have shown. Children and the elderly are particularly vulnerable. This type of pollution also may cause premature births and miscarriages.[251]

Amazon's moving into neighborhoods of color is a new incarnation of an old historical cycle. Amazon builds warehouses on this land because it's cheap. The land is cheap because of patterns of discriminatory policy that have segregrated cities for decades. The presence of loud, polluting warehouses can then lower property values further, starting the cycle all over again. As Quinta Warren says in *Consumer Reports,* when Amazon decides to build warehouses on cheap land in minority neighborhoods, they are "taking advantage of a national legacy of racist policies that have kept cities across the country segregated for generations, and have resulted in disproportionate health and environmental impacts to communities of color."[252] So not only do Amazon's warehouses have a high environmental cost, they can also have a high economic cost despite the promise of jobs and economic "growth." Both kinds of costs—economic and environmental—are paid primarily by people of color.

Of course, Amazon doesn't want you to think about this and it takes steps to make it easier for the average customer to ignore it. For one thing, as we've discussed, the process from clicking "buy now" to the smiling box on your porch is so convenient and fast that it can effectively be ignored. For another thing, while Amazon's warehouses are often in poor neighborhoods of color, Amazon's retail stores like Whole Foods are in wealthy, white neighborhoods. Take my hometown of Cleveland, for example. The first Amazon warehouse I remember seeing is in North Randall, on the site of a now-demolished shopping mall. North Randall's median income is $28,235 and its population is 71% Black. The closest Whole Foods to where I grew up is in Rocky River: $71,636 median income, 95% white. This pattern is repeated anywhere there are both Amazon stores and Amazon warehouses; the wealthy neighborhoods get the flashy stores and the attendant economic benefits. The poor minority neighborhoods get the warehouses and the attendant environmental costs. According to *Consumer Reports*, "On average, just 37 percent of the people who live near Amazon retail facilities are people of color, compared with over half of those who live near its warehouses."[253] There are two ways to be Amazon's neighbor, split along racial lines. If you're a white Amazon neighbor, you're more likely to experience Amazon as the boutique grocery store. If you're Black or Latino Amazon neighbor, you're more likely to experience Amazon as the noisy, polluting warehouse down the street. This racial split outside Amazon's walls is almost exactly reflected within their walls too:

About 19 percent of Amazon employees at the executive level in 2020 were people of color, compared with around 73 percent in warehouse and fulfillment center roles. Those workers in the warehouses are the ones who are at higher risk of injury as climate change increases the likelihood of severe weather events, and they are the ones whose communication is restricted and who don't get to work remotely or take off time when a disaster is coming.[254]

Whether you're an Amazon worker or an Amazon neighbor, you're more likely to bear the brunt of Amazon's environmental impact if you're a person of color. Sacoby Wilson, director of the Center for Community Engagement, Environmental Justice, and Health at the University of Maryland in College Park, says sums it up by saying,

> Communities that host delivery facilities end up being the losers. They get more traffic, air pollution, traffic jams, and pedestrian safety problems, but they don't receive their fair share of the benefits that accrue from having the retail nearby. You can treat this pattern as a form of environmental racism.[255]

The term "environmental racism" was coined in 1982 by civil rights leader Benjamin Chavis, who defined it as

> racial discrimination in environmental policy making, the enforcement of regulations and laws, the deliberate targeting of communities of color for toxic waste facilities, the official sanctioning of the life-threatening presence of poisons and pollutants in our communities, and the history of excluding people of color from leadership of the ecology movements.[256]

Essentially, "environmental racism" can be used to describe any process or policy by which communities of color bear the unfair brunt of environmental risk and destruction, and that definition certainly applies to Amazon. Inside and outside warehouse and retail walls, Amazon is engaged in systemic environmental racism. People of color are disproportionately paying the environmental costs of Amazon's explosive growth, and Amazon is trying to hide these costs from individual consumers.

This is just one way that Amazon is shaping the environment: whole neighborhoods, even whole cities, are split into winner cities and loser cities, often along racial lines. It may seem like the Rocky Rivers are flying, but they're just standing on the backs of the North Randalls. In his remarkable 2021 book *Fulfillment*, Alec MacGillis explores in-depth how Amazon shapes the entire country like this. He writes that Amazon has "segmented the country into different sorts of places, each with their assigned rank, income, and purpose. It had not only altered the national landscape itself, but also the landscape of opportunity in America—the options that lay before people, what they could aspire to do with their lives."[257] If you ask me, that's too much power for a secretive, ruthless, environmentally racist monopoly to have.

Amazon's environmental abuses share a few parallels with their exploitative treatment of their workers: both are huge problems that threaten to shape the national working environment for the worse, both disproportionately affect people of color, and both show signs of hope in the collective organizing of Amazon employees. Like many tech companies, Amazon offers some white-collar employees stock options. In 2018, a group of stock-holding employees presented a shareholder proposal demanding climate accountability at Amazon. It was signed by more than 8,000 of their colleagues. The action was historic; according to the *New York Times*, it was "the first time that tech employees have led their own shareholder proposal."[258] Shareholder activism represented an exciting new front in the battle for a responsible big tech industry, and Amazon was ready to retaliate. Two of the employees, Emily Cunningham and Maren Costa, emerged as leaders of the environmental movement at Amazon, which came to be known as Amazon Employees for Climate Justice. The movement gained momentum, allying with thousands of Amazon employees and inspiring similar groups at other big-tech companies. In September 2019, thousands of Amazon employees joined the Global Climate Strike, a move largely seen as inspiration for the Climate Pledge. The work of Amazon Employees for Climate Justice eventually broadened to include Amazon's workplace conditions and safety. Their efforts drew increasing scrutiny from Amazon, who warned them not to talk to the media about anything related to Amazon.[259] Then, in Covid-ravaged March 2020, Cunningham and Costa "circulated a petition on internal email lists that called on Amazon to expand sick leave, hazard pay and child care for warehouse workers. The petition also asked Amazon to temporarily shut down facilities where workers were confirmed to have the virus so the facilities could be sterilized."[260] A short time later, in April, Cunningham and Costa organized a virtual event for warehouse workers to talk to office workers about safety concerns at fulfillment centers. That was when Amazon decided that enough was enough; soon after the event was announced, Costa and Cunningham were fired. While Amazon's stated reason was that the two worker-activists were fired for "repeatedly violating internal policies" about soliciting coworkers, it certainly seemed like Amazon was trying to quash dissent from an increasingly influential team of activists, much like they fired Christian Smalls after he organized a walkout about coronavirus safety concerns.[261]

The firing of Cunningham and Costa drew immediate backlash, all the way up to several prominent U.S. Senators, who wrote Amazon an open letter seeking "to understand how the termination of employees that raised concerns about health and safety conditions did not constitute retaliation for whistleblowing."[262] Amazon VP Tim Bray resigned in protest of the firing, writing that Amazon's statements explaining Cunningham and Costa's firings "were laughable; it was clear to any reasonable observer that they were turfed for whistleblowing," adding that "remaining an Amazon VP would have meant, in effect, signing off on actions I despised. So I resigned."[263] Eventually, in April 2021, the National Labor Relations Board ruled that Cunningham and Costa were unfairly fired, ordering Amazon to settle with the employees or face charges of discriminatory practices.[264] Of course, transparency-shy Amazon settled, giving Cunningham and Costa back pay and posting notices in workspaces declaring that "Amazon can't fire workers for organizing and exercising their rights."[265] How much Amazon backs up this claim remains to be seen, but one thing is clear: Amazon is finding it more difficult to not only obscure the extent of its environmental impacts, but to dodge accountability for those impacts. Here's hoping that trend continues.

INTERLUDE 7

ON ART, ACTIVISM, AND AMAZON

*P*oet Kevin Killian is the author of seven poetry collections, four novels, one biography, three plays, and over 2,631 Amazon reviews. He has reviewed everything from duct tape to underwear, from push pins to hair straighteners, from Advil to a can of German potato salad. During his lifetime, he was such a prolific reviewer that he was inducted into Amazon's Reviewer Hall of Fame, which is somehow actually a thing. Kevin Killian is known primarily as a poet, a key member of the New Narrative movement of the late 20th century. But he had a prolific shadow career as an Amazon reviewer, and the reviews are wonderful.

Indeed, Killian's thousands of reviews are not straightforward reviews. They're rays of sun in the shadowy crap-land of Amazon's web experience. They burst with humor, vibrant storytelling, and Killian's engaging voice. In one review, for a pair of men's underwear, Killian writes, "Should you manage to get someone to give you these for Christmas, thank them kindly and then make your own way to the dressing room, for it will take you a good 15 minutes for your eyes to stop popping out of your head."[266] In another, for a fake hand, he writes "For years, ever since the shutdown of government support for poetry, Halloween has been a big money making time for us, but in 2011 as I recall we were especially wary of other competition, breathing down our necks, because a good spooky house is something every artist wants to have at his disposal this time of year."[267] It's almost impossible to capture the delight of reading these reviews, or the surprise of finding such wonderful writing in the ad-clogged cesspool of Amazon's website. But that's kind of the point. One way to deal with the oppressive impact of Amazon, tech monopolies, capitalism, or the simple bleakness of modern existence is to try to have some fun with it, if you can. In her introduction to a chapbook compiling some of Killian's reviews, Dora Felix writes,

In misusing this for-profit platform, Kevin Killian joyfully lacerates the supposed doom of the present. The question is not whether to use branded platforms anymore but HOW. Not will we be cash cows but HOW. This gesture, or 2563 gestures, makes a happy vision of the future/present even as the consensual world devolves toward decreasing possibilities for living weirdly.[268]

Seen another way, Killian's reviews attempt to bring dignity into a milieu increasingly dominated by "crapification." In *Art in America*, Kate Durbin writes,

Killian gives the objects he reviews a dignity that the purchasing platform has denied them, as if to suggest they deserve better than adjacency to "buy with one click" buttons and one-star reviews. Killian's reviews are a reminder that capitalism not only objectifies people, but also humiliates objects.[269]

A small group of artists are fighting back against this objectification and humiliation by making art, pranks, and artful pranks about Amazon. Durbin, a poet herself, published *Art in America*'s article "Art about Amazon Expresses Vulnerable Humanity in the Face of a Ubiquitous Behemoth" on March 5, 2020, three days after the first edition of this book came out. I was pretty dismayed to read it at first, simply because it presented such a cool way to look at resisting Amazon, and it came out too late for me to include it in the book. Well, lucky us, here it is. Durbin's piece is fascinating, and I strongly recommend you just go read it. She outlines several artists and their amazing projects. There's Heike Gessler, who wrote *Seasonal Associate*, a challenging and prickly novel about working at an Amazon warehouse in Germany. There's Matt Starr, who wandered the streets of New York carrying a huge pile of Amazon boxes. There's Lauren McCarthy, who installed cameras in (willing) participants' homes and tried to become their own human Alexa. And there's the incredible zine *The Future of Work*, which uses Amazon's MTurk system to generate art. MTurk is, in Amazon's words, "a crowdsourcing marketplace that makes it easier for individuals and businesses to outsource their processes and jobs to a distributed workforce who can perform these tasks virtually." Essentially, companies can hire invisible-to-them workers to do a bunch of online busywork for not very much money. A collective called Anxious to Make, aka artists Liat Berdugo and Emily Martinez, hijacked MTurk to make art. They created a bunch of MTurk surveys to ask these workers all kinds of questions and tasks, from "draw the sharing economy" to "do you have a body?" They then published the results in a zine called *The Future of Work*. In the zine's introduction, Berdugo and Martinez write, "our primary goal is to make artistic works that comment and shape the state of the sharing economy through the systems of this capitalist marketplace itself."[270] Art about exploitative systems made, somehow, within those systems. It's what *The Future of Work* is doing. It's what Kevin Killian was doing with his reviews. It's why I don't particularly mind when this book pops up for sale on Amazon.

Another artist using Amazon's systems to make art about Amazon is Angie Waller, who publishes a series of zines under the imprint Unknown Unknowns. Waller is quite adept at the Amazon-resistance trick of manipulating Amazon's systems into creating art about Amazon. One of her zines, *The Man Who Mistook His Speaker for a Mistress*, collages reviews of Alexa-enabled devices into a sad love story between the devices and the unseen users. In this context, sentences like "I've caught myself missing her while running errands" and "I love how she just waits for instructions" take on strange new resonance that makes the reader question the intimacy people have with these devices. Another of Waller's projects, 2003's *Data Mining the Amazon*, was born from Waller's "creepy feeling" when Amazon's recommendation algorithm served her seemingly-random suggestions, like recommending a Stone Temple Pilots CD after she bought a book about web programming.[271] Inspired, Waller got to work messing with the Amazon algorithm. First, Waller studied user-generated reading lists (from an Amazon feature circa 2000 called "Listmania!"), paying attention to whether each list was created by a self-identified liberal or conservative user. Then, Waller looked at the "users also bought" recommendations for each of the books to see if music skewed political like the books did. *Data Mining the Amazon* is Waller's attempt to use Amazon's recommendation to answer absurd questions like: "is the *Oh Brother Where Art Thou?* Soundtrack a Republican?" Styled like a corporate annual report, filled with graphs and flashy infographics, the project pokes fun at big tech's customer data obsession by making Amazon's algorithms answer absurd questions.[272] In crafting *Data Mining the Amazon*, Waller was ten years ahead of me in raising alarms about the kinds of data Amazon collects, and what it says about its users. Waller's most recent zine is the hilarious and previously-discussed *Grifting the Amazon*, her behind-the-scenes look at how those dodgy self-published ebooks littering Amazon's webstore get made. Reading *The Man who Mistook his Wife for a Speaker* and *Grifting the Amazon*, I didn't know whether to laugh or cry at this universe of overseas ghostwriters, plagiarism, loosely-enforced regulations, lovelorn Alexa users, and cunning passive-income weirdos, all leading to the vast proliferation of the shoddiest books ever published. But I am sure about one thing: Angie Waller is using Amazon to make challenging and compelling art about Amazon.

At some point, the line between making Amazon art and activism blurs. Take Brett Wallace, another artist interested in, among other Amazon-related things, the MTurk. In one memorable project, Wallace made an MTurk task of asking workers to send a picture of their desk, putting a more human face on a process designed to eliminate person-to-person contact. He then installed the photographs on the wall of an art gallery. But Wallace has also been seen at Amazon worker protests, on the front lines of the unionizing efforts in Bessemer, Alabama and Staten Island, New York. It's hard to tell if Wallace's working name, Amazing Industries, describes an artist studio or a think tank. Kate Durbin writes that, "some of the works Wallace presents as part of his Amazing Industries project—the zines and installations particularly—seem more valuable for the information they convey than as artworks."[273] On a similar note, I originally discussed Angie Waller's book *Grifting the Amazon* in this chapter as an art object, but I ultimately decided to move it to Chapter 1 because of its valuable behind-the scenes insight into how Amazon's shoddy self-published books get made. In this vein, according to Durbin, art and activism can and should work together. She writes,

> Direct action aims to make tangible changes in the world. Art creates space for contemplation—a space that can allow for a broader, more sensitive perception of all things. Activism requires both a clear-eyed understanding of how systems of power work and a forceful vision of the future. By offering images of vulnerability, collectivity, and resilience, art can be an indispensable partner in this project.[274]

Art and activism's intersection doesn't have to be limited to large-scale projects like this, either. In October 2019, DJ The Black Madonna dropped out of AWS's Intercept Festival, outraged about Amazon selling AWS tech to ICE.[275] Rapper JPEGMAFIA joined The Black Madonna in dropping out, at the same time 1000 artists were signing a pledge to never perform for an Amazon-related event.[276] In 2021, more than 200 musical artists wrote a letter to beloved Colorado amphitheater Red Rocks demanding the venue stop its use of Amazon's palm-scanning technology at the gates, citing privacy concerns. Red Rocks removed the scanners before the start of the 2022 season.[277] I'm really excited to see more ways art and activism can work together in the fight against Amazon and other big-tech monopolies.

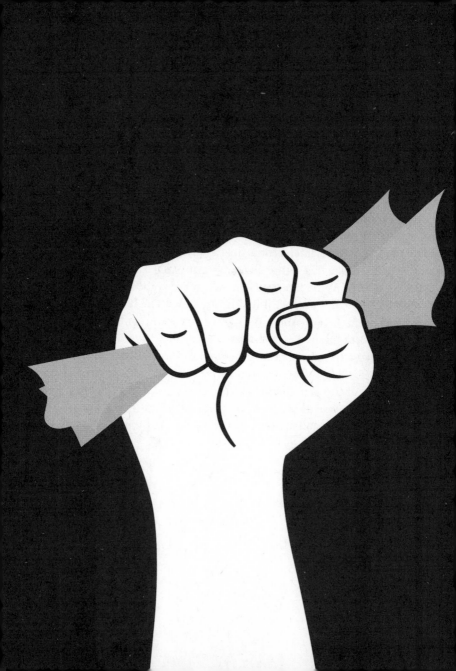

CHAPTER 7

ON AMAZON AND THE GOVERNMENT

*T*t is becoming increasingly clear that one major enabler is allowing Amazon's tremendous growth: the U.S. government. Governments at the local, state, and federal level routinely give Amazon exactly what it wants, and what it wants is tax breaks and permission to be really, really big. Governors, mayors, senators, and representatives regularly issue celebratory press releases proclaiming the good news of new Amazon warehouses, ignoring the fact that the new jobs in those warehouses are grueling and dangerous. Amazon is making inroads at the highest levels of government, a calculated and deliberate move. Amazon can't do what it wants to do without government participation, and all too often governments are willing to play along. But a burgeoning antitrust movement, key Biden administration appointments, proposed new legislation, and a major Congressional investigation may represent a sea change in how the government views monopolizing big tech companies.

On September 7, 2017, Amazon announced that it was on the hunt for a city to host its second headquarters, HQ2.[278] To pick which city would host the new headquarters, Amazon would take proposals from interested applicants. Thirsty for good jobs and good publicity, cities began to fall over themselves to try to attract the attention of Bezos & co. Tweets, promotional videos, and publicity stunts went flying. Billboards were erected. At halftime during an Ottawa Senators home game, the traditional "MAKE SOME NOISE" decibel meter was replaced with a screen that said "Make noise for Amazon."[279] Sidewalk graffiti appeared promising that Calgary would change its name to the awkward "Calmazon." New Jersey planned to hire a plane dragging a banner declaring "cometojerseyjeff.com."

Of course, even more than videos and publicity stunts, cities deployed promises for billions of dollars in tax breaks for Amazon. Much of this was negotiated in secret. Some elected officials didn't even have access to their own city's proposal. When proposals went public, they were heavily redacted. This secrecy hides a massive pipeline between governments and corporations—by some estimates, more than 90 billion dollars in tax breaks goes from cities to lure corporations annually—"more than the federal government spends on housing, education, or infrastructure."[280] Finding legal ways to avoid paying taxes is central to how Amazon does business, and one of their main methods for this evasion is the courting of incentives from local governments. The HQ2 search was an audition for which cities would allow Amazon to avoid paying their share of taxes on their profits.

In the years since I've started advocating against Amazon, it seems the thing that pisses people off the most is the fact that Amazon pays very little or nothing in federal income taxes. People are outraged by the fact that a trillion-dollar corporation pays back so little of it. Maybe it's the fact that we all pay so much in taxes despite not being trillion-dollar corporations. Maybe it's the fact that Amazon asks so much from governments in subsidies, yet pays so little. I don't know, but it makes people mad.

The actual question of whether Amazon "pays taxes" or how much is complicated and, frankly, quite above my head. A few things I know: Amazon pays very little in federal income taxes, taking advantage of loopholes and the fact that they operated at a loss for many years. It's also well known and simple to understand that Amazon resisted charging sales tax on online orders for many years, only as recently as 2017 beginning to actually collect sales tax for purchases in every state that has sales tax laws.[281] Still, it's hard for me to parse the intricacies that lead to a headline like "Amazon paid no federal taxes on $11.2 billion in profits last year" because the tax code is so byzantine and complex, and Amazon is so galaxy-brain adept at manipulating it. Amazon might even be happy that the average person can't grasp what exactly it's doing with taxes. Still, news articles are peppered with sentences like, "By one measure—comparing pretax U.S. profit and the company's "current provision" for U.S. income taxes—Amazon earned $11 billion and had a tax bill of negative $129 million in 2018, essentially getting a net benefit from the tax system."[282] Perhaps illustrative of the problem is this exchange of Tweets from 2019:

Joe Biden: "No company pulling in billions of dollars of profits should pay a lower tax rate than firefighters and teachers."

Amazon: "We pay every penny we owe. Congress designed tax laws to encourage companies to reinvest in the American economy. We have. [. . .] Assume VP Biden's complaint is w/ the tax code, not Amazon."

Amazon unwittingly brings up a good point here: the American tax code is too lenient on billionaires and their massively profitable companies. As demonstrated by Amazon's low tax rates and cities' and states' willingness to give Amazon even more tax breaks and benefits, it's far too easy for companies like Amazon to avoid paying into the governments that permit and encourage their dominance. The watchdog group Good Jobs First calculated Amazon's tax breaks totalling $4.1 billion over the past decade, calling on "on state and local leaders to immediately quit giving tax breaks to the retail giant."[283] Until that happens, in Lawrence, Kansas, a bag of chips is taxed at a higher rate than Amazon pays in federal taxes. Only one of those things is worth more than $1 trillion, and it's not the Doritos.

During the HQ2 search, while municipal marketing budgets and promised tax breaks swelled, Amazon let the data roll in, and by this point we know data is Amazon's favorite thing. Here were hundreds of cities—238, in fact—voluntarily and freely handing over massive troves of data about themselves. Stacy Mitchell, head of the Institute for Local Self-Reliance, was quoted saying "Amazon has a godlike view of what's happening in digital commerce, and now cities have helped give it an inside look at what's happening in terms of land use and development across the U.S. Amazon will put that data to prodigious use in the coming years to expand its empire."[284]

A corporate monopoly like Amazon doesn't just want to be in a city, they want to remake the city in their own image. Seattle, Amazon's home, is a perfect test case of what Amazon wants a host city to look like. According to Alec MacGillis's *Fulfillment*, by 2019, Amazon occupied 20% of the total office space in all of Seattle, more than the next 40 largest Seattle employers combined. This represented a higher share than any other company in any other U.S. city.[285] Amazon remade the entire South Lake Union neighborhood, filling it with such indistinguishable buildings that they required inside-jokey names so that employees would be able to tell them apart.[286] The takeover of South Lake Union was so complete and so bland that a Seattle critical theorist called it a "neo-modern high-tech ghetto."[287] Of course, Amazon isn't happy just taking over Seattle. According to *Jacobin*, "In more and more of the country Amazon acts like an employer in a company town, sucking up whole communities and shaping public goods and services to fit its profit-making needs."[288] Amazon's urban takeovers resemble a tactic from the first era of corporate monopolies: the "company town, in which a monopsony employer effectively becomes the governing structure for public goods and services"[289] When a company like Amazon remakes a city, it's bad news for regular people, whether they work for Amazon or not. Company towns are notoriously exploitative, with companies exercising the staggering control they have over workers' lives by charging unfair prices and dissolving the boundaries between work and life. But if Seattle is any guide, Amazon remaking a city is also bad for everyone else in the city:

> by 2018, the median cost of buying a home, across all home types, was higher in Seattle than anywhere in the country except the Bay Area [. . .] Rent, which had been on par with the national average before 2010, had increased by 57 percent in only five years to more than $2,000 on average, three times higher than the rest of the country.[290]

Where the tech monopolies go, up goes the cost of living, to a point that regular people are priced out of their homes and forced to move into cheaper neighborhoods. Thanks to Amazon's environmental racism, these neighborhoods are of course more likely to have hyper-polluting Amazon warehouses rather than fancy Amazon biospheres. This is the fate of Seattle and the people who used to be able to afford to live there, and it would be the fate of wherever Amazon picked for HQ2.

In the end, Amazon selected Queens and suburban Washington D.C., both of which many viewed as a foregone conclusion. Stacy

Mitchell called the search "a giant ruse," claiming "Amazon is expanding in the nation's two major centers of power, because it intends to envelope, smother and usurp that power for itself."[291] Of the two centers of power Amazon selected, one would welcome it with open arms, and one would chase it away.

Two days after Amazon announced Queens's Long Island City as a winner of the HQ2 sweepstakes, people were already protesting in the streets.[292] A main complaint was the deal's secrecy, with protesters accusing New York of handing out corporate welfare. A broad coalition emerged, led by progressive lawmakers like U.S. Representative Alexandria Ocasio-Cortez, whose district includes the proposed headquarters. After months of protest, testy city council meetings, aggressive advocacy, and passive-aggressive public statements from Amazon, things came to a head in February 2019 when Amazon retracted its plans to move to New York City. Mere months later, Amazon quietly leased 335,000 square feet in New York City's Hudson Yards development, and it plans to employ 1,500 people there. No tax subsidies were required to lure those jobs. Representative Ocasio-Cortez tweeted a picture of herself looking victorious with the caption, "Me waiting on the haters to apologize after we were proven right on Amazon and saved the public billions."[293]

The HQ2 search was a flashy, public, controversial example of Amazon's attempts to ingratiate itself with local, state, and federal governments. But not all of its government ambitions are quite so public. For one thing, Amazon wants to be your city's lone source of office supplies. In 2018, Amazon scored an incredibly lucrative contract with U.S. Communities, "an organization that negotiates joint purchasing agreements for its members, many of which are local governments."[294] The deal is worth billions in supply purchases, with more than 1,500 cities signed on.[295] All this despite the fact that U.S. Communities's bid process was tailor-made for Amazon, and the final contract lacks standard pricing protections, ultimately costing taxpayers more.[296] Beyond office supplies, Amazon is extending its tentacles into government in even more ways. For one thing, it's "aggressively recruiting" former government officials to hire to help them win AWS contracts with big government agencies.[297] Case in point: Amazon spokesperson Jay Carney served as Barack Obama's press secretary. Amazon is also constantly flirting with ICE, trying to score AWS and facial recognition contracts with the shady agency. Amazon even went as far as to purchase a 19.5% stake in Air Transport Services Group, a cargo airline that, among other purposes, runs flights for ICE used to deport immigrants. These "ICE Air" flights are notorious for brutal conditions, described by some as torture (even beyond the torture of forcibly separating immigrants from their communities and families).[298] Speaking of violent colonialist government entities, Amazon has signed a deal with the Israeli Government called Project Nimbus, which will provide AWS server firepower to the Palestine-occupying Israeli Defense Forces.[299] The signing of the Project Nimbus deal was so egregious that an anonymous collective of Amazon employees published an open letter in the *Guardian* demanding that Amazon rescind it; Amazon did not.[300] Amazon even has its eyes on American public education. Since 2019, students at Cajon High School in San Bernardino, CA can take a course called "Amazon Logistics and Business Management Pathway," a series of classes funded by $50,000 in Amazon money.[301] It's important to note that Cajon High School is in the middle of California's Inland Empire, increasingly an Amazon logistics hub and a prominent laboratory for Amazon's company-store urban development strategy. At Cajon, students can sit in a classroom plastered with Amazon slogans like "Customer Obsession" and hear lessons, designed under the tutelage of Amazon consultants, about things like Frederick Taylor's concept of scientific management, a particularly brutal school of worker-efficiency thought from the Industrial Revolution which is a direct antecedent to Amazon fulfillment center's rate-tracking GPS handsets. *Motherboard* obtained class documents from the curriculum. Example questions: "'Why are mergers and acquisitions important to a company's overall growth?' and 'What can Uber do to ensure its competitors are not chipping away at its dominant market share as a result of such bad press?'"

While high school students in California absorbed Amazon-approved corporate talking points in an Amazon-decorated classroom, across the country in Washington DC, a stone's throw from the site of the new Arlington HQ2, finishing touches were underway on a grand mansion. The mansion wasn't being prepared for a politician or a lobbyist or an ambassador or a diplomat.[302] It was being prepared for Jeff Bezos. Only one thing can stop Amazon's seemingly unstoppable expansion and power consolidation: the United States government, and it can do so with laws that are already on the books. So Jeff Bezos, ever playing defense, has turned his attention to Washington.

Standard Oil, American Tobacco Company, the Great Northern and Northern Pacific Railroads: once upon a time, if a single company became too powerful the government would intervene to break it up and preserve the health of the open market. Then, a 1978 book by Robert Bork called *The Antitrust Paradox* changed the entire way the American government viewed antitrust law. Bork, a judge and legal scholar, was instrumental in upending the interpretation of the Sherman Act, the backbone of U.S. antitrust law. In *Monopolized: Life in the Age of Corporate Power,* anti-monopoly advocate David Dayen writes:

> "Instead of an enforcement mechanism to fight market power, Bork argued, the Sherman Act constituted nothing more than a safeguard for "consumer welfare." To Bork, consumer welfare effectively meant lower prices."[303]

Basically, under Bork's ideas, the *only* measure of consumer welfare is low prices. Nothing a company can do, no matter how disruptive or craven, is worthy of Sherman Act scrutiny if the company's actions enable it to lower prices. Mega mergers and corporate consolidation, cause for swift government action in the Progressive Era, no longer raised red flags because of the shift to focus on low prices. Bork's ideas were welcomed by a handsome actor turned politician named Ronald Reagan. As Dayen writes, "the rest was history."[304] One could of course argue that many of Amazon's actions, from the dangerous and underpaid jobs to the environmental racism to the decimating of local economies, are in fact bad for the welfare of consumers. But to Bork, the architect of antitrust thinking for the last 50 years, the ability to buy a copy of *Where the Crawdad Sings* for 75% off is the only measure for the welfare of the consumer. According to this thinking, there's no reason to think about government antitrust action to reign Amazon in.

Yet there are signs that show Bork's blockade is cracking. A new antitrust, anti-monopoly movement is slowly rumbling to life in America. Of course I feel it, having sold more than 10,000 copies of a little pamphlet about resisting Amazon. But the Amazon resistance movement isn't just from the literary world. Pressure to reign in tech monopolies is building all over, from Capitol Hill to the nation's best law schools.

As much as a law student can be a star, Lina Khan was one. As much as an article journal can go viral, her "Amazon's Antitrust Paradox" did, with a nod to Robert Bork right there in the title. When it appeared in *The Yale Law Journal*, it rocketed her to relative fame, with appearances on NPR and profiles in *The New York Times* and *The Atlantic*. I appreciate Kahn's outspoken anti-Amazon work because it fills in gaps where I'm not qualified to speak. I'm happy to discuss Amazon's effect on culture and bookstores; in *The Atlantic*, Khan says, "There's a whole line of critique about Amazon that's culture-based, about how they're wrecking the experience of bookstores. I personally am less focused on that element."[305] Khan focuses instead on interpretation of antitrust law. The abstract of "Amazon's Antitrust Paradox" claims, "the current framework in antitrust—specifically its pegging competition to "consumer welfare," defined as short-term price effects—is unequipped to capture the architecture of market power in the modern economy."[306] Robert Bork, in other words, was not prepared for something like Amazon. Khan's point is that we need to reinvent antitrust thinking by "restoring traditional antitrust and competition policy principles" to better deal with Amazon.[307] And now Khan is at the center of the government's first real chance to do so in a generation: in 2021, Joe Biden named Lina Khan the chairperson of the Federal Trade Commission. It's an incredibly influential position, and it may well afford her a chance to enact some of her antitrust philosophy through policy and regulation. Matt Stoller, a leading anti-monopoly thinker, called Khan's appointment "earth-shattering."[308] Khan, the youngest-ever head of the FTC, was aggressive out of the gate. Within the first few months after her appointment, Khan had

> re-filed an aggressive antitrust complaint that the F.T.C. had initiated in 2020, seeking to break up Facebook. In September, the agency published a report analyzing hundreds of acquisitions made by the biggest tech companies which were never submitted for government review. Although the report didn't call for any specific action, it was a sign that Khan intends to look far deeper into Big Tech's business than her predecessors did.[309]

Adding to the earth-shattering nature of Khan's appointment is the broader idea that the Biden administration is making a sharp turn away from his former boss's tech-friendly attitude. While Barack Obama was happy to let big tech do whatever it wanted to, Biden is showing signs he wants "to reshape the role that major technology companies play in the economy and in our lives."[310] There's Khan's appointment, for one thing. Biden has also appointed other noted new-antitrust thinkers to key administration roles as well, notably Tim Wu in a spot on the National Economic Council and Jonathan Kanter as Assistant Attorney General of the DOJ's Antitrust Division. Khan, Wu, and Kanter are such exciting appointments for antitrust nerds that a website called LeftyGoods made coffee mugs featuring a "Wu & Khan & Kanter" design.

These Biden administration moves and appointments represent some of the most significant government attempts at antitrust reform that we've seen in decades. Antitrust is having a moment—some call it the "New Brandeis Movement," some call it "Hipster Antitrust," I call it exciting. I'm hopeful that some good policy may actually come from this. We couldn't have arrived here without the tireless work of so many advocates like Stacy Mitchell. The co-director of the nonprofit Institute for Local Self Reliance, Mitchell believes "no corporation is above the law" and that "If we don't regulate Amazon, we are effectively allowing it to regulate us."[311] Mitchell and the ILSR are doing important work, including helping to found Athena, a labor-focused coalition designed to advocate for the breaking up of Amazon. According to David Streitfeld, Mitchell's 2016 report "Amazon's Stranglehold: How the Company's Tightening Grip Is Stifling Competition, Eroding Jobs, and Threatening Communities," combined with Khan's "Paradox," provide "a road map for a new, more critical approach to the e-commerce colossus."[312] Persistent and vocal and visible, Mitchell is also optimistic about possible changes in antitrust enforcement. Streitfeld quotes her as saying, "Things that were inconceivable a few years ago are now being discussed. The antitrust argument against Amazon is much more alive than the antitrust argument against Walmart ever was. There's a sense that we have to fix inequality or it will be the country's undoing. I'd hate to give up on this moment."[313] Lina Khan has echoed Mitchell's thought that we're in an unprecedented moment: in 2011, when she went to work for Barry Lynn's trailblazing anti-monopoly think tank Open Markets Institute, Khan says "It definitely felt like we were on the margins of the policy conversation."[314] Now, thanks to her new job and some like-minded officials in the Biden Administration, Khan is directly in the center of an exciting new policy conversation.

One place the antitrust hipsters can look for possible ways forward is Europe. Amazon is rapidly expanding there, and they already represent a huge share of the European e-commerce market. While Amazon is expanding around the world, Europe is where its American strategy is being repeated most faithfully:

> Some of the company's outposts around the world feature limited selections geared toward digital products that Amazon can sell without expensive physical infrastructure, but the European operations are much like those in the U.S.— with networks of fulfillment centers, legions of third-party merchants selling their wares on the site and full-fledged Prime memberships offering two-hour delivery in more than 20 European cities.[315]

If Amazon is going to replicate its U.S. dominance anywhere, it'll probably happen in Europe first. Some Europeans are worried about it, too: *How To Resist Amazon and Why* from France, England, Germany,

Switzerland, and Ireland (and outside of Europe and the U.S., the book has also made its way to Malaysia, Thailand, and Australia).

But Amazon's welcome in Europe isn't without bumps. For one thing, the European Union will be the first to levy actual antitrust charges against Amazon. The charges, the result of a two-year investigation, "stem from Amazon's dual role as a marketplace operator and a seller of its own products [. . .] In them, the EU accuses Amazon of scooping up data from third-party sellers and using that information to compete against them, for instance by launching similar products."[316] In November 2021, Amazon began an effort to settle the with the EU to stave off huge fines, but it was unclear whether the effort would be successful (for instance, Google has tried and failed to settle antitrust charges from the EU).[317] While the result of these negotiations about the specific antitrust charges remains uncertain, one thing is clear: The EU is planning on enacting serious new antitrust regulations to curb big tech's power as soon as Spring 2023.[318]

Another key difference between Europe and the U.S. is that labor unions in Europe have been more successful at reigning in Amazon than American unions have: "At home, Amazon faces much weaker unions than it does in Europe, where participation hovers close to 23% on average compared with about 10.3% in the U.S. While union membership has declined over the past couple of decades in France and Germany, worker groups can still disrupt or force companies into talks."[319] This has led to strikes, increased pressure on Amazon, and the total shutdown of its French operations. After the French government, facing union pressure about worker safety, ruled that Amazon could only sell "essential goods" during the Coronavirus pandemic, Amazon responded simply by closing its French fulfillment centers.[320]

France's government has long been pro-small business in ways the American government hasn't. For instance, during the Coronavirus pandemic, "France's government has repeatedly called on consumers stuck at home to buy from domestic e-commerce companies rather than the Silicon Valley giant."[321] Contrast that with American cities falling over themselves to offer Amazon tax breaks, or Obama administration officials flocking to big tech jobs after his administration ended. The French government has also propped up the French book industry in ways that have left French bookstores more equipped to weather the Amazon storm. France is one of thirteen European countries that legislates maximum discounts on the price of books; for much of Europe, Amazon selling books at anything more than 5% off would be illegal, thus leveling the playing field.[322] In 2021, despite fierce lobbying by Amazon, France took another step by passing a law setting a minimum shipping charge for books, a move widely seen as protecting bookstores from Amazon's loss-leader free shipping.[323] The Paris city government even subsidizes independent bookstores. Because of these protective measures, France has more bookstores than the United States despite having just 20% of America's population.[324] Interestingly, while a significant majority of American households have Amazon Prime accounts, only 40% of French households do.[325] European strategies, from actual antitrust action to strong unions to policies prohibiting predatory pricing, represent a possible way forward for curbing Amazon's power in the United States.

There's hope: as of this writing, both Houses of Congress have investigated big tech's business practices, including Amazon. Perhaps Jeff Bezos, ever responsive to public pressure, felt this growing pressure when he decided on Washington D.C. as the location for the new headquarters. Or his purchase of *The Washington Post*. Or that mansion. The biggest private residence in Washington, D.C., in fact. A residence with "191 doors (many either custom mahogany or bronze), 25 bathrooms, 11 bedrooms, five living rooms/lounges, five staircases, three kitchens, two libraries/studies, two workout rooms, two elevators—and a huge ballroom."[326] That ballroom is key. Bezos put roots down in the capitol to make friends with legislators—legislators who may be hearing from these antitrust hipsters in the Biden Administration. Legislators who may be asking questions of Bezos in hearings for the big tech antitrust investigations. In the PBS *Frontline* documentary *Amazon Empire: The Rise and Reign of Jeff Bezos*, Stacy Mitchell says the house "has a big ballroom. I mean, it is designed to create a real presence for him in the nation's capital, where he can hobnob with the people who make decisions."[327] Bezos clearly has his eyes on the nation's capital, the very place where any successful action to break up his company must originate.

There are signs that Jeff Bezos's reception in Washington DC won't be as warm as he hopes. Recall the April 2020 *Wall Street Journal* report found that "Amazon employees have used data about independent sellers on the company's platform to develop competing products."[328] Of course, this is the practice that led to the antitrust charges from the European Union. Thing is, Amazon has already denied doing this in Congressional testimony. The anti-competitive practices are only one of the House Judiciary Committee's concerns; the other being that Amazon lied to Congress. Congressional response was outraged and, more importantly, bipartisan. "Sen. Josh Hawley (R., Mo.) pushed the Justice Department to open a criminal antitrust inquiry into the company" While "Democrats on the judiciary panel questioned whether Amazon misled Congress in sworn testimony from July."[329] Mere days after the *Wall Street Journal* report, the House Judiciary Committee sent Jeff Bezos a letter compelling him to testify about the report's allegations. The letter, signed by Democrats and Republicans, claimed in part that,

> If these allegations are true, then Amazon exploited its role as the largest online marketplace in the U.S. to appropriate the sensitive commercial data of individual marketplace sellers and then used that data to compete directly with those sellers.

It sounded like something Stacy Mitchell would say. Indeed, Mitchell celebrated the "notably bipartisan" letter, writing, "Amazon often acts as though it's above the law. Today, the House Judiciary Committee firmly demonstrated that it's not."[330]

We know that antitrust enforcement is an uphill battle thanks to Robert Bork and Ronald Reagan's long shadows. Still, the House Judiciary letter made other accusations that are perhaps more clear-cut. The letter reads, "If the reporting in the *Wall Street Journal* article is accurate, then statements Amazon made to the Committee about the company's business practices appear to be misleading, and possibly criminally false or perjurious." Just a few short months after moving into his new party house, instead of sending out exclusive invitations, Jeff Bezos received one of his own.

The party didn't appear to be very fun for Mr. Bezos. When the antitrust subcommittee finally held their big tech hearing with Jeff Bezos and CEOs from Google, Facebook, and Apple on July 30th, 2020, Bezos stammered and dodged a surprisingly robust line of questioning. Many observers agreed it was a uniquely sharp Congressional hearing that had the CEOs, Bezos included, on defense. The CEOs were so caught off guard and the committee was so prepared that, Franklin Foer writes, "With many of their questions, members seemed to know the inner workings of the companies better than their executives," though the execs could've easily been feigning ignorance as a strategy.[331] That strategy represented a short-term gain, long-term hassle for Bezos; in March 2022, a House Panel recommended the DOJ investigate Amazon for lying during the investigation, indicating that Amazon "conceal[ed] the truth" and that charges of Obstruction of Congress might be in order.[332]

Still, despite the possible obstruction, the committee got enough out of the CEOs to represent what could be the beginning of an exciting new chapter in U.S. antitrust enforcement. Writing in *The American Prospect,* David Dayen claims "It's amazing what a little evidence and a set of politicians committed to their job can do. And it raises the bar, both for the ability for Congress to conduct oversight, and for Washington to do something about the relentless power of Big Tech."[333] Franklin Foer agreed, saying "Congress gets kicked so often for doltish preening that it seems a great miracle when it actually does its job. David Cicilline, the Rhode Island Democrat who chairs the subcommittee, has conducted a master class in how to frame an issue and then press a case for action."[334] The invigorated and well-prepared committee scored plenty of points against the bumbling, uncertain tech CEOs. For instance, one line of questioning about the Diapers. com acquisition caused Jeff Bezos to basically admit that predatory pricing was part of Amazon's strategy; he called it a "traditional idea." He also refused to deny that Amazon employees had stolen proprietary information from third-party products to make competing Amazon-label products.

All in all, subcommittee chair David Cicilline made perhaps the loudest-yet case for breaking up big tech. David Dayen attributes this newfound antitrust energy to a familiar face: Lina Khan, whom Cicilline hired as a counsel to the subcommittee before she got promoted to FTC Chair. It paid off: Khan's persuasive arguments about the unfairness of Amazon serving as platform and competitor simultaneously were all over the hearing. It was a breath of fresh air to see Congresspeople, in a televised hearing with a huge audience, knowledgeably asking the same questions that we Amazon resisters have been asking for years. In a stirring statement about halfway through the hearing, Cicilline declared, "The evidence we've collected shows that Amazon is only interested in exploiting its monopoly power over the e-commerce marketplace to further expand and protect its power. This investigation makes it clear that Amazon's dual role as a platform operator and competing seller on that platform is fundamentally anticompetitive and Congress must take action."

In October 2020, Cicilline's subcommittee issued their report, and the hearings were only a preview of the strong case he'd make for government action to curb big tech monopoly power. The Republicans on the committee refused to sign the report, caught up in their outrage about alleged anti-conservative bias from big tech. Still, it's a major legislative achievement, a throwback to a time when Congressional investigations were robust and productive. Even briefly, antitrust issues got a national spotlight in the breakneck insanity of the late-2020 news cycle. Much of the country was paying attention as David Cicilline, in the final report's introduction, laid out clearly and simply that Amazon, Google, Apple, and Facebook "wield their dominance in ways that erode entrepreneurship, degrade Americans' privacy online, and undermine the vibrancy of the free and diverse press. The result is less innovation, fewer choices for consumers, and a weakened democracy."[335] The statement could serve as a thesis for everything up until now in this book. Most encouragingly to me, the subcommittee suggested Congress act to update the Robert Bork-influenced consumer welfare/low prices standard of antitrust law; the report "recommends that Congress consider reasserting the original intent and broad goals of the antitrust laws, by clarifying that they are designed to protect not just consumers, but also workers, entrepreneurs, independent businesses, open markets, a fair economy, and democratic ideals."[336] Amen to that.

•   •   •

When I finished the first edition of this book, I didn't know who would win the 2020 presidential election. The part right up there about the Antitrust Subcommittee report was the last part I wrote, and I snuck it in under my deadline's wire. While the report represented a significant achievement in the nascent antitrust movement, it felt strange to wonder if it'd all evaporate in a few months. Well, I'm excited to append this chapter with that rarest of government commodities: good news. First, it's worth reiterating how important it is to antitrust reform progress that people like Lina Khan, Jonathan Kanter, and Tim Wu have high-ranking jobs in the Biden administration. Second, the Antitrust Subcommittee s report led to the introduction of five bipartisan-sponsored bills to the House of Representatives. Each bill would go a long way towards solving important issues explained in this book. A quick summary of the package of bills, each co-sponsored by a Democrat and a Republican:

1. The American Innovation and Choice Online Act (AICOA) would make it illegal for a company to "self-preference" their own products in online marketplaces that they run. Essentially, Amazon would no longer be able to exploit the platform/competitor loophole to prioritize their own products.

2. The Platform Competition and Opportunity Act would make it illegal for companies like Facebook to acquire upstart competitors in order to gain monopolizing market share. Facebook's acquisition of Instagram is one example.

3. The Ending Platform Monopolies Act would make it illegal for big tech companies to own another line of business that represents a conflict of interest. The bill works by "removing the ability and incentives of a dominant platform to use its control over multiple business lines to preference itself and disadvantage competitors." If passed, this bill could lead to the break-up of Amazon.

4. The Augmenting Compatibility and Competition by Enabling Service Switching Act forces companies to let you take your data with you when you switch a service, and ensures the data is standardized so it works across platforms. Even if this bill doesn't pass, it's mere specter has already done a little bit of good. Apps like Facebook now make it easier to grab your data and pictures before you quit.

5. The Merger Filing Fee Modernization Act boosts funds for antitrust enforcement agencies by making it more expensive for huge companies to file merger applications.[337]

In June 2021 all five bills advanced out of the House Judiciary Committee.[338] As of this writing, they have yet to face a full House vote. But in January 2022, the Senate Judiciary committee advanced their version of AICOA on a strong bipartisan vote.[339] It remains to be seen if the bill will get a full vote in either chamber, but many view the AICOA as the best shot at new antitrust legislation due to its bipartisan support in both House and Senate Judiciary Committees.[340] Further, antitrust momentum may be picking up in state houses as well. The Twenty-First Century Antitrust Act is currently working its way through the New York State Senate and Assembly. The Institute for Local Self-Reliance says the bill has "incredible momentum;" as of this writing, the bill has passed out of committee in the New York Senate, and it has collected 30 cosponsors in the Assembly. The bill is a checklist of New Brandeis priorities, including merger reforms, revisions to "abuse of dominance" standards, the elimination of abusive non-compete clauses, and increased ability for workers and small businesses to band together and hold monopolies accountable. Alas, it seems as if I'll have to turn in this draft before I know whether any of these bills ever pass. Such is the peril of trying to write an up-to-the-minute nonfiction book during a nationwide book printing shortage (a shortage caused, of course, by corporate consolidation). So I'll just leave with this takeaway: three years ago, when I started this project, progressive antitrust reform still seemed like a fringe idea with little political will. Now, the Biden Administration has a powerful trio of antitrust innovators in influential positions, and meaningful bills to prevent Amazon's marketplace exploitation are crawling through both chambers with bipartisan support. We've come a long way. Here's hoping, by the time you read this, we've gone further.

INTERLUDE 8

ON DELIGHTS

In memory of Stanley DeFries, 1928-2021

*H*ere's just a little of the non-economic, unmeasurable stuff that's at stake if Amazon's dominance makes more small businesses go away. Not super high stakes, of course. But people would miss it if it was gone. A lot of Amazon's impact is economic. But not all of it.

A customer this afternoon, call her Emily, was buying a book for a second time because she had loaned it to a friend. Emily wasn't sure she was going to get the book back but she loved it so much that she had to make sure she had a copy. "I might also loan this one out and come see you again," she said at check out. Emily then told me a story about a friend recommending a book. Emily's friend said that the book had been passed from friend to friend to friend, and now it was coming to Emily because her friend loved it so much. Upon opening it, Emily realized that it was in fact her book that she had loaned out ages ago. It had bounced from person to person and finally was coming back home.

As people buy travel guides, we sometimes ask them about their upcoming trips. The more far-flung the better. We sell a lot of *Rick Steves London* but just today we sold a folding paper map of Panama and a copy of *Lonely Planet Egypt*.

Today Mary told me she placed another review in the IndieNext List. She's worked here for just over a year and I think it's her fifth IndieNext review.

Customers who are so excited about the fancy art book they special ordered that they take it out of the shrink wrap right there and open it up on the counter to show us.

When I'm back in the office putting orders together and I can hear Chris and Nikita cracking each other up as they unpack boxes.

When I'm handselling and I offer a customer four choices and they buy all four.

Honestly, just handselling at all.

When a customer buys my book and doesn't realize I, the author, am ringing up the transaction. The face they make when I ask if I can sign it.

Ngaio, the shop cat, gets in a lap-sitting mood when the weather gets colder. She sits right between the fiction and nonfiction rooms and stares at incoming customers, often emitting tiny meows. She then turns around and walks towards the couch. If someone follows her and sits on the couch, she'll instantly jump on their lap and stay there until forced to move. I've walked into Nonfiction countless times to see a customer happily trapped. Some people give me a look that says "this is fun but I kind of need to get to this thing in ten minutes and I don't want to upset this precious tiny old lady cat." I tell them to just stand up because if they try to lift her off their lap, no matter how purring and docile she seems, they will get bitten.

When grandparents bring small kids to the store and say yes to every "can I have this book?"

When you have the Saturday opening shift and the store is quiet and the cats are eating and the sunlight slants in through the windows. A sunny Saturday morning is the best time to work at a bookstore. When I was still part-time at The Raven and I had the Saturday morning shift I used to dream about owning the store.

When someone comes in knowing exactly what they want and they find it.

When someone comes in not knowing what they want at all and they find it.

When someone comes in and heads right to poetry and stays there for an hour.

When someone browses so happily for so long you forget they were even in here to begin with.

Unbeknownst to each other, two people are reading the *Wheel of Time* series at the same time. They both special order a book in advance, so they pick one up and order the next one right there like someone really strategizing at Red Lobster's Endless Shrimp. They were neck and neck for a while but now Rob is pulling ahead. Last time Rob was in, picking up book 15 or something, he pulled a sonogram out of his wallet to show me, beaming with pride.

When Chris sees the parking meter person coming and yells for me, giving me just enough time to grab quarters and dash out the door.

The moment, ten minutes before an event starts, when you realize you'll need more chairs.

People who shop off the staff picks shelf.

A woman drove all the way from Oklahoma City to see our Karin Slaughter event at the Topeka Library. She wore a tee shirt that said "I GOT SLAUGHTERED." I wasn't there for her visit to the store but Nikita told me about it later when I came to pick up the books for the event. I saw the Slaughter superfan at the event, sitting in the front row 45 minutes early. I walked up to her and said "are you from Oklahoma City?" and she said "How did you *know?*"

When our point of sale system crashes it displays a warning: "Cannot redefine THIS"

There are maybe two weeks a year when the weather is right for keeping the door open. Any given day when the door is open the cats are uninterested in running outside for a total of about 20 minutes. Those minutes.

Stanley and Alice Jo stopping by after lunch. They always tell us where they went to lunch. These days sometimes Stan feels like staying in the car but he always waves.

One time Stanley and Alice Jo came in after lunch (Free State Brewing Company) and they brought a painting of the Raven that a local artist had made. It's a closeup of our facade with a red Subaru parked out front. Sitting on our bench, somehow, is a man wearing a very large hat. That painting.

Ilya Kaminsky came to town recently to read his amazing poetry. The day after the reading I took him to KU to visit Megan's class, then I drove him to Topeka for his afternoon events at Washburn. That car ride. He kept trying to buy me lunch. "I already ate!" I declared. Ten mintues later he said "are you sure I can't buy you something to eat?" He also kept asking how he could help our store. He wouldn't believe me when I told him he already had.

CHAPTER 8

HOW TO RESIST AMAZON

*T*his is not a book about the individual consumer's need to boycott Amazon. I have chosen to divest entirely (as much as humanly possible) from this company, and you may feel like you want to do the same. But, as the previous chapter outlines, the problem of Amazon is a government problem, and it needs a government solution. The last thing I want to do is police people's buying habits or economic decisions. I'm not here to shame you out of your Amazon Prime subscription. I am here to educate you on what Amazon does to communities, workers, bookstores, and small businesses, and I'm here to politely ask you to call your representatives to tell them antitrust reform is important to you.

This is also not a book about me trying to get rid of my business competition. Yes, I sell books. Yes, Amazon sells books, too. Yes, Amazon is the biggest threat to my ability to keep selling books. But I assure you that isn't what this is about.

In many ways, Amazon isn't my competition at all. Indie bookstores have long leaned on what they do best to deal with bigger competition. It worked during the heyday of the chain megastores, and it may very well work during the age of Amazon. Many people in the book industry think bookstores will survive by focusing on their strengths and creativity. They say that thinking about Amazon as competition at all isn't productive. After all, is a 1,200 square foot creaky bookstore really in the same league as a trillion-dollar corporation with a highly advanced logistics, shipping, and cloud computing network?

Rather than try to eliminate any business competition, I write this book instead to do what I can to protect a way of life I value. A way of life that has nurtured me and many I know. This way of life promises that someone with a good idea can start their own business. That person can provide good jobs to people in their community, they can take inspiration from serving that community, they can give back to their community, they can keep that community's money circulating within that community. It's a way of life where the little league team has the name of a locally-owned business on the back of their jerseys. Where charity and school silent auctions are absolutely brimming with gift cards donated by local businesses. Where customers can be greeted by name when they enter a store or restaurant. Where restaurants can serve food grown in the same zip code. I'm not just being wishy-washy or nostalgic. A 2022 report by the British think tank Institute of Place Making found that "Booksellers significantly contribute to the vitality and viability of their high streets" and "booksellers are actively engaged in driving change and support in their local communities."[341] But this isn't even just about bookstores. It's about hardware stores and restaurants and bars and taxes and the environment and the USPS and unions and privacy and the government and local control. Resisting Amazon is bigger than bookstores. Resisting Amazon is about protecting communities.

Ever since I even thought about committing any of this to paper by making the first version of the *How to Resist Amazon and Why* zine, I've used language of "resistance" and not "boycotting." One simple reason for this choice is that it's very hard to actually boycott Amazon, which is part of my complaint about them. Your dollar is your vote, and Amazon has made it very difficult for any Internet user to vote against them. Their cloud computing and web services businesses mean anyone that regularly uses the Internet is probably contributing to Amazon's profits. Amazon helps host places like Netflix, they host ads across the Internet, and their embedded links pepper the faces of millions of websites. This seems to be one of the most profitable parts of their business. It is also the part that makes their business hard to boycott. For instance, according to one cloud computing consultant, the top ten biggest users of AWS are Netflix, Twitch, Linkedin, Facebook, Turner Broadcasting, BBC, Baidu, ESPN, Adobe, and Twitter, while other companies who've publicly acknowledged using AWS include the USDA, Canon, Expedia, Capital One, *The Guardian*, Harvard Medical School, General Electric, Johnson & Johnson, Lyft, McDonald's, NASA, Nokia, Pfizer, Reddit, Yelp, and Zillow among more than a million others.[342] My whole anti-Amazon story really got going when a tweet thread I wrote about Amazon's book pricing went viral. That thread probably used Amazon server power to get to all those eyeballs.

Still, like I said, your dollar is your vote. While your purchasing of a Margaret Atwood book from an independent bookstore instead of Amazon won't make much of a difference for Amazon, it could be the difference between a profitable day and an unprofitable day for the indie bookstore. If you're discouraged by how massive and impossible to avoid Amazon is, think instead of how to support your local small businesses in the face of Amazon's dominance. Gestures that feel small compared to Amazon's might will be huge for us. Don't vote *against* them, vote *for* small businesses. With that in mind, consider these ways to resist Amazon.

1. Shop Local

The most important way to resist Amazon is to take the money you would've spent in Bezos's empire and spend it instead at local, independently-owned small businesses. Even better if those businesses are unionized, pay a living wage, or do things like offer cooperative ownership. Shopping at these places has a tremendous effect on those businesses and your communities. Somewhere between 50 and 75 percent of money spent at local small businesses stays in your community, and the percentage for Amazon purchases can be much, much lower—sometimes as low as 0.

But again, this is about more than money. A robust network of creative, responsive, community-oriented small businesses is anathema to Amazon's view of the world; in fact, it's the opposite of Amazon's global conquest. My hometown is Cleveland, Ohio, and towards the end of my time there an explosion of craft breweries rippled across downtown. The first big new brewery, Market Garden Brewery, opened across the street from Great Lakes Brewing Company. Great Lakes had been the neighborhood's only microbrewery for decades; surely they were frightened by a big new competitor yards away. Nope. Their response in the local media amounted to "a rising tide raises all ships."[340] This community spirit is absent from anything Amazon values; Amazon's model is to either purchase competing businesses, or to simply copy their ideas and sell them cheaper until the innovator is forced to shutter. Because of tech monopolies, innovation at startups has ground to a halt.[344] While tech innovation struggles under big tech's shadow, community-oriented small business craft brewers have driven an explosion of craft beer. Collaboration and partnership are exactly what Amazon doesn't stand for. Collaboration and partnership are built into the values of many small businesses.

2. Cancel Your Prime Subscription, or even better, your Amazon account

Amazon Prime makes it easier for you to give money and data to Amazon. The free 1-day shipping is a tremendous incentive for people to click the purchase button. It's so tremendous that Amazon almost certainly loses money on many of these transactions. But what it loses in shipping costs it gains in data: Prime members not only share their purchasing, browsing, listening, and streaming data with the world's most valuable company, they *pay* to do it. Remember, as Rena Foroohar writes in *Don't Be Evil*: "*People* are the resource that's being monetized. We think we are the consumers. In fact, we are the product."[345]

To cancel your Prime subscription, log in to your account, then select "Your Prime Membership" from the "Account & Lists" drop-down menu. On the left side of the screen, you'll see "End Membership and Benefits" as an option. Click the link, and then confirm that you want to cancel your membership."[346]

While it's pretty easy to cancel your Prime subscription, it's much harder to cancel your Amazon account. Even without a Prime account, Amazon can still mine your data, as long as you have an account you use to make purchases. No account means no products and, more importantly, no data. Amazon doesn't want you to exist outside of their data-sucking system, so they've made deleting your account a multiple-hoops-to-jump-through process. To close your Amazon account, you have to submit a request first, then respond to a message Amazon sends you within five days. To send a request, go to https://tinyurl.com/229auyrr and follow the instructions. When Amazon sends you the message asking to confirm, make sure to confirm.

3. Avoid Amazon-affiliated brands

It's a simple and clear first step to resisting Amazon: stop spending money at Amazon.com. But, like many mega-corporations, Amazon has an ever-growing portfolio of subsidiaries and acquisitions. To resist Amazon, resist spending money at these Amazon-controlled or -owned companies as well:

- AbeBooks
- Audible
- Goodreads
- IMDb
- PillPack
- Ring
- Twitch
- *The Washington Post*
- Whole Foods
- Zappos

Additionally, Amazon purchased entertainment giant MGM in 2021. A moviemaking giant founded in 1924, MGM has a massive portfolio of properties that includes all the James Bond movies, *Wizard of Oz*, the Rocky films, and countless others. From here on out, every time you see that beribboned lion roaring at the beginning of a movie, Jeff Bezos is making money. The average consumer probably doesn't keep track of which studios make which movies, which is likely fine by Amazon. Again, boycotting is difficult here because watching an MGM movie or even visiting a website where one of Amazon's companies has an ad technically counts as contributing to their bottom line. But still, there are independent small business-friendly alternatives, which I'll discuss in the next section.

Another way to resist Amazon: avoid Amazon-produced TV shows and entertainment. Aside from MGM's massive portfolio, the following is a small selection of entertainment produced directly by Amazon-controlled companies:

- The *Good Omens* TV adaptation
- *Jack Ryan*
- *The Marvelous Mrs. Maisel*
- *Transparent*
- *Bosch*
- *The Grand Tour*
- *Fleabag*
- The *The Underground Railroad* TV adaptation
- *The Lord of the Rings: The Rings of Power*
- *Leverage: Redemption*

In addition to Prime Original TV shows like the ones listed above, several publishing imprints including Thomas & Mercer Publishing, Lake Union Publishing Company, and Little A Publishing are owned by Amazon. Current TikTok-popular author Colleen Hoover has published multiple books with Montlake, an Amazon imprint.

4. Instead of Amazon-affiliated brands, use indie-friendly alternatives

Fortunately, Amazon isn't the only company producing television, books, or the services mentioned above. Amazon wants you to think that they're the only place to buy things online. I fear what happens if the word "Amazon" becomes a stand-in for "online shopping" the way "Kleenex" has become a stand-in for "tissue." One way to resist Amazon is to remember that there are other companies doing everything they do.

Instead of Amazon-controlled companies, consider supporting the below small business-friendly alternatives:

- For used or rare books use Alibris.com
- For audiobooks use Libro.fm
- For books, shop direct from independent bookstores or use bookshop.org, which donates a portion of sales to independent

bookstores. Bookshop.org also has an affiliate linking program that pays more than Amazon's, and has been picked up by several national outlets.

- For information about movies and actors, use Wikipedia

- Instead of a subscription to *The Washington Post*, consider subscribing to your local newspaper, which needs your help more than ever. Or, rely on publicly-funded news sources like NPR or PBS.

- For organic groceries, shop at a farmer's market, sign up for a CSA, or become an owner at your local food co-op.

- Buy shoes from a locally-owned independent shoe store, many of whom sell online in case there isn't one in your city or town.

- The StoryGraph is a new online book review database that could end up being a long-needed alternative to Goodreads—and provides more useful information for readers, like content warnings.

In terms of streaming entertainment, things are a bit more complicated. Netflix is a competitor to Amazon Prime but relies on Amazon's AWS to manage its tremendous traffic. Disney+ is also an alternative, but many may feel the same way about Disney that I feel about Amazon. Additionally, it's very difficult to tell which streaming services or websites use AWS. There's no master database of AWS customers, likely because that's proprietary information Amazon would like to keep quiet. In 2018 a web plugin popped up that allegedly blocked all AWS content, but once it's loaded it provides a "remarkable view of the internet at large. Entire services are missing, so you won't be able to listen to Spotify, book a flight on Expedia, or look at rooms on Airbnb. Even where websites load, there may be holes punched out of them — missing images, embedded apps, or entire ad networks."[347]

In the end, the case of using the internet in the age of AWS is another example when it's easier to take a positive stance. Rather than completely avoid AWS, which may be impossible for any serious internet user, you could make a choice to purposefully support independent streaming services and media. Even if that means you're using Amazon's server capacity, at least you'll be supporting cool folks doing cool stuff independently of large corporations. Consider your public library—many public libraries provide streaming alternatives for TV, movies, ebooks, and audiobooks for card members. I've been using Kanopy and Hoopla, both of which are free with my library card. Public libraries are one of the last great anti-capitalist spaces. To really resist Amazon and what they represent, form a good and loyal relationship with your public library.

5. You don't have to plug your house into Amazon's privacy-invading security network

Throughout this book I've (hopefully) made the case that what Amazon wants most from you is your data: you are not their customer, you are their product. I've hopefully also shown that people should think twice about trusting Amazon with that data. Much of this data comes from tracking browsing and purchasing habits of shoppers, which you can avoid by resisting shopping on Amazon. But even more of this data comes from people who voluntarily *pay* to place data-collecting devices inside their homes. They do this by purchasing Alexa-enabled devices and Ring security doorbells. One of the most important ways we can resist Amazon is by keeping them out of our homes. Jeff Bezos has many extravagant homes, including the largest private residence in the nation's capital city; he doesn't need control or access to your house, too.

6. Advocate

When you spend money on something, the transaction is about more than you exchanging your money for some goods or service. That money is also a de facto endorsement of the business you're giving it to. By giving money to a business, like it or not, you're telling that business that you approve of the way they do things. One way to resist Amazon, other than (of course) not buying things from them, is to instead give money to businesses whose practices are better than Amazon. A bit of research can help you find businesses with unionized workers, businesses with high wages, employee-owned businesses, and businesses who work to reduce their impact on the environment. This is a form of advocacy you can enact every day. Call it wallet advocacy.

There's also more traditional advocacy. You can do things like write to your representatives in support of the government's antitrust investigations into Amazon and other big tech companies. Contacting your representative is a much less laborious task than it used to be. Apps like Resistbot allow you to contact your rep with a simple text message. Many think tanks, coalitions, and organizations in the fight against tech monopolies host tools on their websites that make contacting your reps as easy as possible. For instance, on the website of one anti-Amazon coalition, Athena, the very first thing you see is a link to sign a petition to Congress.

Speaking of Athena, traditional coalition-building and organizing against Amazon has ramped up in recent years, too. Athena is a labor coalition spearheaded by the Institute for Local Self Reliance aiming to curb Amazon's power and abuses. You don't even need to go to a meeting; even following groups like Athena on social media, or signing up for their email lists, is a small step towards resisting Amazon.

Social media has also made it easier to stand in direct solidarity with Amazon workers attempting to force change from the inside. People like Christian Smalls advocating for coronavirus safety measures and trying to unionize Amazon warehouses, or groups like Amazon Workers For Climate Justice, can get their message directly to you through social media. You can in turn amplify it. It's easier than ever to stand in solidarity with these workers, and though Amazon tries to silence or fire them, they will not be quieted, especially if they get the social media audience they deserve.

I will say here that the book industry is far from perfect in many of these regards. My industry is not above critiques of worker mistreatment. Too often the romance of working in the book industry is used as a way to manipulate its workers into accepting less money and benefits. The thinking goes that because workers are so *lucky* to work in *books*, they should be happy to take lower salaries and fewer benefits. I try to embrace the joy of working in this business (and there is still joy) without using it to bludgeon people into working for less than they deserve.

It's not hard to imagine that, if the company responsible for most of all book sales drives down prices and demands steeper discounts from publishers, less money will flow into the book industry. It's also not hard to extrapolate that less money flowing into the industry means less money to pay workers, and it's rarely the executives that suffer when wages need to be reduced. The people who feel wage pinching are always the entry-level workers. If Amazon selling books for lower prices means less money for publishers to pay entry-level workers a living wage, that's a problem. If CEO salaries swell while interns go unpaid, that's a problem. Part of the reason I joined the American Booksellers Association board of directors in 2021 was to advocate for entry-level book industry employees. Part of the reason I'm writing this book is to fight for a book industry that celebrates the joy of books *and* pays a fair living wage to every one of its workers, no matter the job title or experience. Our industry needs to be strong enough to not let Amazon dictate how it does business. Our industry should not, at any cost, take cues on how to treat workers from Amazon.

One way you can help fight for this equitable *and* joyful book industry is to vote with your dollar. Whenever you support the book business, you can support bookstores and publishers that value their workers. They're out there, though there should be more. One of the factors preventing there being more publishers and bookstores paying their workers what they deserve, I argue, is Amazon. They are by far the single company with the biggest influence on the book industry. They are also the single company working hardest to devalue the book. Simple logic leads to the conclusion that Amazon is working to make less money flow into the book industry. When less money flows into any given industry, the first people to suffer are the people at the bottom of the ladder. In devaluing the book, Amazon is working to devalue the people who work with books, too.

7. Make art about and outside of Amazon

Every revolution has its fighters and its artists. For every Christian Smalls, there's an Angie Waller. Both are important. Making art about Amazon (or corporate abuses or monopolies or trying to be human in a late-capitalist world) is one way to capture hearts and minds and point people towards action and fighting for change. If anything in this book makes you feel strongly, well, strong feeling is a place that art comes from. My art about Amazon comes in the form of zines and books, but who knows what form yours will take. Remember, as Kate Durbin writes, "art can be an indispensable partner in this project."

Another note about art: while the self-publishing revolution had the potential to break down traditional gatekeeping in publishing, Amazon's purchase of CreateSpace and their transforming it into Kindle Direct has simply created another gatekeeper. Yes, "independent" authors are no longer dependent on corporate publishers, but a huge percentage of them are instead dependent on Amazon, who prints, distributes, ships, and otherwise controls their books. It doesn't have to be this way. All you need to publish a zine is access to a photocopier and a long-arm stapler, which you can get for 30 bucks. You don't even need a computer! Making your own zine means Jeff Bezos and company can never touch what you create. That's how this whole project started: a zine I made in my living room. Once people got interested in the zine and I ran out of time to make them all, Microcosm stepped in to help distribute them. Microcosm, of course, doesn't do business with Amazon at all. So I managed to write a zine and sell tens of thousands of copies of it without using Amazon services or giving them any money at all. Amazon wants you to think they're the only way to self-publish; they aren't. They can't take your stapler.

8. Make it known

Since this project began I've heard some funny stories. Fed up with how many Amazon boxes showed up at her apartment building, one person ordered ten copies of the zine, enough to slip under each apartment door. Another person was horrified to hear that their family's Secret Santa gift exchange would have an Amazon theme. Their entry into the exchange was a copy of this book, wrapped inside a discarded Amazon box. Mind you, this kind of thing can go wrong, and I'm not encouraging people to get preachy. But I do encourage people to have conversations about Amazon's abuses of workers, the environment, communities, and small businesses. It's an important discussion to have; one of my first goals when beginning this project was to break the Amazon Discussion out of its closed bookseller-to-bookseller cycle. There's lots of evidence that this book has successfully created bookseller-to-consumer discussions. Now, I'd love to see consumer-to-consumer discussions about Amazon. You don't have to be preachy or condescending or mad. It's a tricky balance, and I don't always get it right. But I do think it's an important discussion to have. Again, I'm not suggesting you become the Prime Police (gosh, please don't) but discussions can be a good thing. The solution to the Amazon problem is a macro, policy solution, but that doesn't mean consumers can't have discussions among themselves about it. Remember, Amazon wants to trap you in their system. They want to make it so convenient to use Amazon that you don't even think about it. Maybe one conversation is all takes for someone to begin thinking about it.

9. You can't scare me, I'm sticking to the union

As of this writing, something that at once seemed impossible has taken place: an Amazon warehouse has voted to unionize. Even more surprisingly, the union that will represent the warehouse is an upstart independent union founded by former Amazon employees, and it ran an unconventional campaign that upended a lot of conventional wisdom about unionizing. The Amazon Labor Union is maybe the biggest of all the David vs. Goliath stories about Amazon. A brand new startup facing one of the world's most valuable companies, and Goliath is gearing up to do absolutely everything it can to stop this David. The good news? You can help David.

One of the most important ways to resist Amazon is to support the workers who are on the front lines trying to end Amazon's abusive work environment through unionizing, and there are lots of ways to help a union from the outside. For one thing, you can simply follow them on social media (@AmazonLabor on Twitter, @amazonlaborunion on TikTok and Instagram) or sign up for their mailing list. When you like or retweet or share their posts, it not only exposes your followers to important content, but it also helps ALU content bust through those pesky algorithms. The ALU also has a Gofundme running; donating money will help them campaign in other warehouses, and endure the brutal legal fight Amazon is preparing. Plus, unions always need money to pay their members if they go on strike. ALU has also announced plans to launch a merch shop with shirts and other gear made at unionized print shops. Buying union merch not only helps fund union efforts, but it raises visibility when you wear it out and about. Supporting the Amazon Labor Union is literally funding the resistance; these are the folks fighting hardest to make Amazon a better place to work.

I'll reiterate one more time that, while it's the most prominent example, Amazon is simply one of many places in need of reform to treat workers better. There's a lot of evidence that union activity is picking up across the board; in general, if you care about worker's rights, it's a good idea to seek out unionized businesses to support. The above ways to support Amazon's union are good for all unions.

An important note: always follow the union's lead when looking to support them (this is one reason why it's so helpful to follow them on social media). When you see a company engaging in brutal union-busting tactics, it's an understandable impulse to boycott that company. But a boycott may cause the union to lose leverage, because the company can then say the union is bad for business. Often, the union will share what it thinks are the best ways to support it—for instance, when Politics and Prose bookstore unionized in December 2021, in the face of massive resistance from store owners, the union asked customers to wear red when they visited the store to show their support. They also urged authors not to cancel events, because doing so would cast the union in a negative light and complicate negotiations with ownership. Workers do need your support, but they're the experts on how you can best do that. It really seems like something is happening; it was once pretty unthinkable to imagine union activity ripping through places like Amazon or Starbucks. A reinvigorated labor movement has the potential to not only make Amazon a better place to work, but America a better place to work.

10. Dream of a Level Playing Field

A world where Amazon plays by the rules is possible. A world where small businesses are robust, creative, and everywhere is possible. A world where one can earn a living wage and build a career working at a bookstore is possible. A world where large technology companies can be trusted with our data is possible. A world where one company no longer has a chokehold on the entire publishing industry is possible. A world where billionaires and their incredibly profitable companies pay their fair share of taxes is possible. Hell, a world without billionaires is possible. An Amazon-controlled future is not a given. Many things need to happen to create this future. Government action is necessary, but do not underestimate the power of collective individual action too.

CHAPTER 9

CONCLUSION

So what's the big deal? Amazon is just one company. There have been big companies before and there will be big companies again. The death of the American small business has been declared many times, allegedly murdered by everything from the shopping mall to Walmart. Yet the American small business persists. Many headlines even claim that independent bookstores are having a renaissance. So why does Amazon need to be resisted?

I would argue that Amazon is actually unlike any big company before it. Even if it's using old tricks, no company has done all of this to quite this scale. No company has ever been the cloud computing backbone of much of the Internet *and* built a private surveillance network connected to thousands of police departments *and* created the world's largest online marketplace *and* built its own shipping network from the ground up *and* tried to single-handedly stamp out a nascent labor movement *and and and*. The list goes on. Amazon does so much so relentlessly. It has turned itself into one of the world's most valuable companies in the process. Here's the thing about successful companies: their success makes other companies want to emulate them. If we let Amazon keep going, they're going to rewrite the rules simply by virtue of other companies trying to emulate Amazon's model. If the rules are rewritten with Amazon as the idea of success, many people will be left out.

Warehouse workers will be left out. Labor unions will be left out. Third-party contractors risking injury and life for a company without being considered actual employees will be left out. Small businesses will be left out. Heck, the idea of brick and mortar retail might even be left out, forever altering the landscape of our cities and towns. People trying to minimize the supply chain's impact on the environment will be left out. Allowing Amazon to rewrite the rules of the economy will be catastrophic for workers, the planet, and Amazon's competitors.

Lest you think I'm overreacting (or simply lashing out at a competitor for my business), I'd remind you that time and time again Amazon has shown that its ambitions are global (or even bigger than global) in scale. Watching them and researching them over the course of this book, it seems to me that they're not content to turn a nice profit for their shareholders. Rather, it seems like they want to reinvent home surveillance. It seems like they want to build a replacement for the United States Postal Service. It seems like they don't want to be the biggest online marketplace; rather they want to be the *only* online marketplace. In *The Atlantic*, Franklin Foer concludes that Jeff Bezos

> assumes roles once reserved for the state. His company has become the shared national infrastructure; it shapes the future of the workplace with its robots; it will populate the skies with its drones; its website determines which industries thrive and which fall to the side. His investments in space travel may remake the heavens. The incapacity of the political system to ponder the problem of his power, let alone check it, guarantees his Long Now. He is fixated on the distance because he knows it belongs to him.[348]

Is the fight to resist Amazon hopeless? I'm not actually sure, but I for one won't go down without a fight.

After I posted my letter to Jeff Bezos on Twitter, someone replied to call me naive, saying that blacksmiths bemoaned the advent of Henry Ford's Model T, that typewriter manufacturers complained about the advent of the IBM personal computer.

I have two responses to this accusation. First, I ask if Amazon actually represents progress. Does unprecedented corporate consolidation and power actually signify steps to a better future? The IBM computer was a revolutionary tool that enabled the democratization of human knowledge. On the other hand, Amazon's unchecked expansion in many ways threatens democracy. I mean, come on: they're building their own shipping infrastructure, surveillance network, and court system. So before anyone accuses me of trying to stand in the way of progress, take a minute to consider what progress really is or can be. Do we want a future where billionaires, by simple virtue of their riches, are granted governing power?

My second thought is this: the blacksmith is good at his job. He serves his community. He has found a way to make a living with a useful skill. Who would expect the blacksmith to quietly endure a threat to his livelihood? Do we expect him not to protest the Model T? Do we automatically accept the Model T and all the beliefs of its problematic inventor? Does the blacksmith ignore the dangerous implications of the Model T way of doing things? Even if he can't win, who would ask the blacksmith to be quiet? I may just be the c0-owner of a small bookstore in the middle of the country trying to argue against the world's richest man, but that doesn't mean I'm going to quietly watch the world's richest man relentlessly collect money, influence, and power.

I believe in a future where workers are well paid and have power over their circumstances and environments. I believe in a future where small businesses are vital contributors to their communities. I believe in a future where commerce takes into account its environmental impact. I believe in a future where the government is driven by the will of its citizens, not the business interests of its richest constituents. I believe Amazon is working to derail that future.

APPENDIX
FOR FURTHER READING

This book is designed to be an introduction to government, privacy, environmental, and labor issues concerning Amazon. It is far from comprehensive, and there's much more I could've said. I also finished the first draft of the second edition in March 2022, and things can happen very quickly, so I'm sure a lot has happened since I sent this off to the folks at Microcosm for publication. Point being: if you're interested in resisting Amazon, start with this book, but continue with the real experts.

I wanted to make sure to ground this book in my bookstore owner perspective; I am not an investigative journalist and I didn't want to try to force myself to become one to write this book. Fortunately, lots of good investigative journalists have gone into much more depth about the issues in this book. The following is a list of resources I used in the writing of this book, as well as places you can find more thorough investigations about these issues.

Amazon's Systemic Impact
MacGillis, Alec. *Fulfillment: America in the Shadow of Amazon.* New York: Picador, 2021.

> Alec MacGillis's thesis in *Fulfillment* is a compelling one: the combined effect of Amazon is literally shaping our national landscape. As Amazon expands and builds, it's creating winner cities (Seattle) and loser cities (Dayton). *Fulfillment* is a rich, narrative nonfiction look at Amazon full of compelling stories and original reporting.

Anticompetitive Practices
Berzon, Alexandra, Shane Shifflett, and Justin Scheck. "Amazon Has Ceded Control of Its Site. The Result: Thousands of Banned, Unsafe or Mislabeled Products." The Wall Street Journal. Dow Jones & Company, August 23, 2019

> *The Wall Street Journal*'s investigation into counterfeit products on Amazon looks into the dangers of bootleg products on Amazon, yes, but it's also a clearheaded look into how Amazon manipulates sellers and customers with its dual platform/competitor business model.

Mattioli, Dana. "Amazon Scooped Up Data From Its Own Sellers to Launch Competing Products." The Wall Street Journal. Dow Jones & Company, April 24, 2020.

> This is the investigation that got Jeff Bezos a letter inviting him to testify on Capitol Hill. The investigation finds that Amazon stole ideas from sellers on its platforms to create its own Amazon-branded products. Amazon executives are on the record telling Congress that they did nothing of the sort. The evidence in this investigation suggests otherwise.

West, Emily. *Buy Now: How Amazon Branded Convenience and Normalized Monopoly*. Cambridge, Massachusetts: The MIT Press, 2022.

> West's book wisely and comprehensively investigates exactly how Amazon got so big. We have a huge monopoly controlling many parts of our lives, to the point that it's basically infrastructure, and West's book is a valuable investigation into how Amazon got there and stays there.

Antitrust Law

Khan, Lina M. "Amazon's Antitrust Paradox." The Yale Law Journal, January 2017.

> This is the article that galvanized a nascent antitrust movement and landed its young author in the pages of *The Atlantic*. Khan's article outlines a clear need to rethink antitrust law interpretation in the face of a company like Amazon.

Mitchell, Stacy, and Olivia LaVecchia. "Report: Amazon's Stranglehold: How the Company's Tightening Grip on the Economy Is Stifling Competition, Eroding Jobs, and Threatening Communities." Institute for Local Self-Reliance, November 29, 2016.

> Stacy Mitchell's report, cited in David Streitfeld's *New York Times* profile of her (itself worth reading), clearly outlines the Institute for Local Self Reliance's arguments against Amazon. ILSR and Mitchell are two powerful voices in the fight against Amazon's dominance.

Dayen, David. *Monopolized: Life in the Age of Corporate Power*. New York: The New Press, 2020.

> Dayen's book frames its study of corporate power around case studies, an innovative approach that brings attention to the human cost of corporate consolidation and power. His thesis is that, even beyond Amazon, monopolies touch every corner of American life and business.

Stoller, Matt. *Goliath*. New York, NY: Simon & Schuster, 2019.

> Matt Stoller's *Goliath* is a history of antitrust enforcement in the United States. It's a helpful look at a time when the government wasn't hobbled in its ability to reign in the power of too-large companies.

Wu, Tim. *The Curse of Bigness: Antitrust in the New Gilded Age.* **Columbia Global Reports, 2018.**

> Wu, now an economic advisor to President Joe Biden, outlines the lessons from the first Brandeis movement and uses them to outline a course for the second.

Bookstores

Deutsch, Jeff. *In Praise of Good Bookstores.* **Princeton University Press, 2022.**

> Deutsch, a good friend of mine and director of Chicago's nonprofit Seminary Co-op Bookstore, makes a thoughtful philosophical case for the protection of what he calls "good bookstores."

Gregory, Chris; Dr Regine Sonderland Saga; and Professor Cathy Parker. *Booksellers as Place-Makers: The Contribution of Booksellers to the Vitality and Viability of High Streets.* **Institute of Place Management, 2022.**

> This British report does good work quantifying the economic and non-economic impact of bookstores on high streets. Spoiler alert: bookstores are really good for towns.

Labor Practices

Labor reporters Kim Kelley and Lauren Kaori Gurley are doing fantastic up-to-the-minute work on the new labor movement in the U.S. One of the best parts of their reporting is their focus on talking to the workers affected by and shaping the labor movement. By the time you read this, Kelly's new book *Fight Like Hell: The Untold History of American Labor* will be out. I haven't read it, but I am excited to do so.

Stone, Brad. *The Everything Store: Jeff Bezos and the Age of Amazon.* **New York, NY: Back Bay Books/Little, Brown and Company, 2018.**

> Stone's book is the only biography of Jeff Bezos and a valuable insight into the mind of Amazon's founder. In 2021, he released a sequel called *Amazon Unbound*, also worth reading.

Guendelsberger, Emily. *On the Clock: What Low-Wage Work Did to Me and How It Drives America Insane.* **New York, NY: Back Bay Books/Little Brown & Company, 2020.**

> Aside from being the most thorough on-the-job-at-Amazon narrative I found, Guendelsberger's book is a crucial study of how low wage work affects one's mind, body, and life.

Evans, Will. "Prime Labor: Dangerous Injuries at Amazon Warehouses." Reveal, November 25, 2019.

> *Reveal's* reporting on Amazon's injury rates, timed perfectly to release on Black Friday 2019, went a long way to puncture the myth that Amazon's warehouse work is just as grueling as any other warehouse work. In fact, it's more dangerous. *Reveal* was named a Pulitzer Prize finalist for this work.

Privacy

Zuboff, Shoshana. *The Age of Surveillance Capitalism: the Fight for a Human Future at the New Frontier of Power*. New York: PublicAffairs, 2020.

> Nobody has gone deeper on the cost of big tech's data obsession than Zuboff does in this monumental book.

Frontline Empire: The Rise and Reign of Jeff Bezos. PBS. Public Broadcasting Service, 2020.

> The 2020 *Frontline* documentary is invaluable for its quick summation of all the issues surrounding Amazon's dominance, but to me the most chilling part was its footage of a child's Ring-enabled baby monitor being hacked.

Foroohar, Rana. *Don't Be Evil: How Big Tech Betrayed Its Founding Principles--and All of Us*. New York, NY: Currency, 2019.

> Foroohar's book is a useful exploration of many issues surrounding the explosive growth of big tech, which she argues was founded with nobler intentions that have been abandoned.

Shipping

Leonard, Devin. *Neither Snow nor Rain: a History of the United States Postal Service*. New York, NY: Grove Press, 2017.

> Leonard's history of the U.S. Postal Service explains its resiliency and importance, as well as how, in later years, Amazon pushed it around and betrayed it with false promises.

Allen, Joe. *The Package King: a Rank-and-File History of UPS*. Chicago, IL: Haymarket Books, 2020.

> Allen's new union history of the UPS includes discussion of Amazon's effect on yet another pillar of the global logistics network

O'Donovan, Caroline. "The Cost of Next-Day Delivery: How Amazon Escapes The Blame For Its Deadly Last Mile." BuzzFeed News, September 6, 2019.

> O'Donovan's Buzzfeed investigation on Amazon's shipping is shocking, well-reported, and essential.

Part of the challenge of writing this book is how quickly things change. Social media is essential in keeping track of things, and it's a valuable way to connect directly with the activists and Amazon employees working to improve things.

Acknowledgments

A portion of this book appeared on LiteraryHub under the title "Did Amazon Throttle My Sales After I Criticized Them in the *New York Times*?" Several of the interludes first appeared, in different forms, as installments of the Quoth The Raven email newsletter.

Thank you to The Raven's booksellers for being such a joy to work with, and being so inspiring in creating an image of what a bookstore can be: Adela, Chris, Christina, Hannah, Sameah,Wulfe, Jack, Kahill, Kami, Kelly, Lily, Manda, Mary, Nancy, Nikita, and Sarah. Thank you to Ben Cartwright in Spokane and Suzanne DeGeatano at Mac's Backs for both, in their own ways, encouraging me to turn my online anti-Amazon advocacy into something in print. Thank you to PBR Writers' Club (Julia, Rachel, Chance, Maggie, Will, Jon, and Althea) for reading parts of this book and also helping staple zines when we were still doing things that way. Thank you to Joe at Microcosm for taking a leap of faith in the original zine version of this project and encouraging me to write this version, and thanks to Elly and Lydia and everyone else at Microcosm for doing such amazing work on this book and all the others. Finally, thank you to Kara and Jack for a million kinds of support.

Cited Sources

1. "Amazon Empire: The Rise and Reign of Jeff Bezos," PBS (Public Broadcasting Service, 2020), https://www.pbs.org/wgbh/frontline/film/amazon-empire/transcript/.

2. Brad Stone, The Everything Store: Jeff Bezos and the Age of Amazon (New York, NY: Back Bay Books/Little, Brown and Company, 2018), 25

3. Ibid., 26

4. Stacy Mitchell, "Report: Amazon's Toll Road," Institute for Local Self-Reliance, March 3, 2022.

5. Alex Shephard, "Can Amazon Finally Crack the Bestseller Code?," The New Republic, January 16, 2020, https://newrepublic.com/article/156228/can-amazon-finally-crack-bestseller-code.

6. Didi Tang, "Amazon Agreed to Allow Only Five-Star Reviews for Xi's Book in China," *The Times* (The Times, December 20, 2021)

7. David Streitfeld, "What Happened to Amazon's Bookstore?," The New York Times (The New York Times, December 3, 2021)

8. Carolyn Kellogg, "Amazon and Hachette: The Dispute in 13 Easy Steps," Los Angeles Times (Los Angeles Times, June 3, 2014), https://www.latimes.com/books/jacketcopy/la-et-jc-amazon-and-hachette-explained-20140602-story.html.

9. Judith Rosen, "Authors Pen Open Letter to Amazon About Hachette Dispute," PublishersWeekly.com, July 3, 2014, https://www.publishersweekly.com/pw/by-topic/industry-news/bookselling/article/63180-over-300-authors-ask-amazon-to-settle-hachette-dispute.html.

10. Margot Boyer-Dry, "Welcome to the Bold and Blocky Instagram Era of Book Covers," Vulture, January 31, 2019, https://www.vulture.com/2019/01/dazzling-blocky-book-covers-designed-for-amazon-instagram.html.

11. Ibid.

12. Jim Milliot, "Judging a Book by Its Title," PublishersWeekly.com, February 7, 2020, https://www.publishersweekly.com/pw/by-topic/industry-news/bookselling/article/82381-judging-a-book-by-its-title.html.

13. Nausicaa Renner et al., "Smorgasbords Don't Have Bottoms," n+1, February 26, 2020, https://nplusonemag.com/issue-36/the-intellectual-situation/smorgasbords-dont-have-bottoms/.

14. Jim Milliot, "Amazon Reducing Orders to Publishers," PublishersWeekly.com, November 11, 2019, https://www.publishersweekly.com/pw/by-topic/industry-news/bookselling/article/81708-amazon-reducing-orders-to-publishers.html.

15. Strategic Organizing Center, "COMPLAINT TO THE FEDERAL TRADE COMMISSION BUREAU OF CONSUMER PROTECTION Washington, D.C. Against AMAZON.COM, INC. for Unlawful Deception under Section 5 of the Federal Trade Commission Act, 15 U.S.C. 45 (a)." December 8, 2021.

16. Streitfeld, "What Happened?"
17. Ibid
18. Angie Waller, *Grifting the Amazon* (New York: Unknown Unkowns, 2021)
19. Ibid
20. Anne Trubek, "This (Amazon Third-)Party Is Getting out of Hand," (Notes from a Small Press, December 7, 2021)
21. Barry C. Lynn et al., "Killing the Competition, by Barry C. Lynn," Harper's Magazine , December 29, 2021
22. Sara Ashley O'Brien, "Here's Why Amazon and Instacart Workers Are Striking at a Time When You Need Them Most," CNN (Cable News Network, March 31, 2020), https://www.cnn.com/2020/03/30/tech/instacart-amazon-worker-strikes/index.html.
23. Paul Blest, "Leaked Amazon Memo Details Plan to Smear Fired Warehouse Organizer: 'He's Not Smart or Articulate'," Vice, April 2, 2020, https://www.vice.com/en_us/article/5dm8bx/leaked-amazon-memo-details-plan-to-smear-fired-warehouse-organizer-hes-not-smart-or-articulate.
24. Ibid.
25. Russell Brandom, "After Walkouts, Amazon Pledges Temperature Checks and Masks in All Warehouses," The Verge (The Verge, April 2, 2020), https://www.theverge.com/2020/4/2/21204254/amazon-warehouse-walkout-coronavirus-protections-masks-temperature.
26. Sara Saracsalinas, "Amazon Raises Minimum Wage to $15 for All US Employees ," CNBC (CNBC, October 2, 2018), https://www.cnbc.com/2018/10/02/amazon-raises-minimum-wage-to-15-for-all-us-employees.html.
27. "How Much Does Jeff Bezos Make per Minute?," The Independent (Independent Digital News and Media, October 13, 2021)
28. Hillary Hoffower, "We Did the Math to Calculate How Much Money Jeff Bezos Makes in a Year, Month, Week, Day, Hour, Minute, and Second," Business Insider (Business Insider, January 9, 2019), https://www.businessinsider.com/what-amazon-ceo-jeff-bezos-makes-every-day-hour-minute-2018-10.
29. Nick Statt, "Amazon Is the Ruthless Corporate Juggernaut People Love," The Verge (The Verge, October 27, 2017), https://www.theverge.com/2017/10/27/16552614/amazon-popularity-user-survey-prime-echo-trust.
30. Maryam Mohsin, "10 Amazon Statistics You Need to Know in 2020 [Amazon Infographic]," Oberlo, January 15, 2020, https://www.oberlo.com/blog/amazon-statistics.
31. Emily Guendelsberger, On the Clock: What Low-Wage Work Did to Me and How It Drives America Insane (New York, NY: Back Bay Books/Little Brown & Company, 2020), 23.
32. Ibid., 22, 23
33. Ibid., 41
34. Ibid., 22
35. Ibid., 59
36. Ibid.
37. Ibid.
38. Matt Day and Benjamin Romano, "Amazon Has Patented a System That Would Put Workers in a Cage, on Top of a Robot," The Seattle Times (The Seattle Times Company, September 7, 2018), https://www.seattletimes.com/business/amazon/amazon-has-patented-a-system-that-would-put-workers-in-a-cage-on-top-of-a-robot/.
39. Guendelsberger, On The Clock, 20
40. About Amazon Staff, "Amazon's Fulfillment Network," About Amazon, May 8, 2018, https://www.aboutamazon.com/working-at-amazon/amazons-fulfillment-network.
41. Guendelsberger, On The Clock, 112
42. Will Evans, "Ruthless Quotas at Amazon Are Maiming Employees," The Atlantic (Atlantic Media Company, January 21, 2020), https://www.theatlantic.com/technology/archive/2019/11/amazon-warehouse-reports-show-worker-injuries/602530/.
43. Ibid.
44. Michael Sainato, "'I'm Not a Robot': Amazon Workers Condemn Unsafe, Grueling Conditions at Warehouse," The Guardian (Guardian News and Media, February 5, 2020), https://www.theguardian.com/technology/2020/feb/05/amazon-workers-protest-unsafe-grueling-conditions-warehouse.
45. Ibid.
46. David Dayen, Monopolized: Life in the Age of Corporate Power (New York: The New Press, 2020), 197.
47. @ grimkim on Twitter, December 22, 2021
48. Lauren Kaori Gurley, "Warren, Sanders Demand Investigation into Amazon's Attendance Policy," VICE, March 3, 2022
49. Will Evans and Rachel de Leon, "How Amazon Hid Its Safety Crisis," Reveal, June 30, 2021
50. Ibid.
51. Ibid.
52. Ibid.
53. Weise, Karen, and Eric Berger. "At Amazon Site, Tornado Collided with Company's Peak Delivery Season." The New York Times. The New York Times, December 12, 2021.
54. "Our Facilities," About Amazon, September 21, 2020
55. Clark Randall et al., "Workers Are Dying Because Amazon Treats Human Beings as Disposable," Jacobin, September 1, 2022
56. Sophie Hurwitz, "Amazon Warehouse Workers Want to Feel Safe," The Nation, February 17, 2022
57. Randall et al, "Dying"
58. Ken Klippenstein, "After Deadly Warehouse Collapse, Amazon Workers Say They Receive Virtually No Emergency Training," The Intercept, December 13, 2021
59. Laurel Deppen, "New Reports Examine Amazon's Strained 'Employment Machine' and Alleged Race Problem," GeekWire, June 15, 2021
60. Spencer Soper, "Deadly Collapse at Amazon Warehouse Puts Spotlight on Phone Ban," Bloomberg.com (Bloomberg, December 11, 2021)
61. @MorePerfectUS on Twitter, 13 December 2021
62. @davehclark on twitter, 11 December 2021
63. Weise and Berger, "Amazon Site"
64. Hurwitz, "Workers"
65. Shepardson, David. "U.S. Sends Hazard Alert Letter To Amazon

After 2021 Fatal Warehouse Collapse." Reuters, April 26, 2022.

66. Dayen, Monopolized, 198

67. Ken Klippenstein, "Documents Show Amazon Is Aware Drivers Pee in Bottles and Even Defecate En Route, despite Company Denial," The Intercept, March 25, 2021

68. Lauren Kaori Gurley, "Amazon Delivery Drivers Can Be Fired for Peeing in Bottles," VICE, February 11 2022

69. Ibid.

70. Caroline O'Donovan, "The Cost of Next-Day Delivery: How Amazon Escapes The Blame For Its Deadly Last Mile," BuzzFeed News, September 6, 2019, https://www.buzzfeednews.com/article/carolineodonovan/amazon-next-day-delivery-deaths.

71. Guendelsberger, On the Clock, 16

72. Dayen, Monopolized, 192

73. Ibid.

74. Ibid. 201

75. Steven Greenhouse, "Workers at an Amazon Warehouse Reject Forming a Union," The New York Times (The New York Times, January 16, 2014)

76. Lauren Kaori Gurley, "Secret Amazon Reports Expose Company Spying on Labor, Environmental Groups," Motherboard (Vice News, November 23, 2020).

77. Ibid.

78. Ibid.

79. Sara Morrison, "How a Mailbox Could Get the Amazon Union Vote Overturned," Vox (Vox, May 21, 2021)

80. Grace Pezzella and Sejal Singh, "What Amazon Got Away With," Slate Magazine (Slate, April 13, 2021)

81. Ibid.

82. John Logan, Sharon Zhang, and Candice Bernd, "Amazon Is Paying Consultants Nearly $10,000 a Day to Obstruct Union Drive," Truthout (Truthout, March 9, 2021)

83. Ibid.

84. Pezzella and Singh, "Got Away"

85. Olivia Solon and April Glaser, "Fired, Interrogated, Disciplined: Amazon Warehouse Organizers Allege Year of Retaliation," NBCNews.com (NBCUniversal News Group, March 30, 2021)

86. @MorePerfectUS on Twitter, February 16, 2021

87. Solon and Glaser, "Fired"

88. Pezzella and Singh, "Got Away"

89. Morrison, "Mailbox"

90. Ibid.

91. Ibid.

92. Ibid.

93. Jason Del Rey, "Amazon Has Won a Historic Warehouse Union Election. but the Battle Is Not over.," Vox (Vox, April 9, 2021)

94. Jon Brodkin, "Amazon's Anti-Union Conduct Made Free Election 'Impossible,' NLRB Officer Finds," Ars Technica, August 3, 2021

95. Ibid.

96. William Thornton, "Amazon apparently wins second Bessemer union vote count."Alabama.com, March 31, 2022

97. Jodi Kantor and Karen Weise, "How Two Best Friends Beat Amazon," The New York Times (The New York Times, April 2, 2022).

98. Ibid.

99. Ibid.

100. Lauren Kaori Gurley, "The Amazon Labor Union Took On America's Most Powerful Company—and Won" Motherboard (Vice, April 4, 2022)

101. Lauren Kaori Gurley, "Watch: NYPD Arrests Amazon Union Organizers at Staten Island Warehouse," VICE, February 23, 2022

102. Ibid.

103. Ibid.

104. Lauren Kaori Gurley, "Amazon Labor Union Is Inspiring Amazon Workers Around the Country to Unionize" Motherboard (Vice, April 14, 2022)

105. Andrea Hsu, "Starbucks workers win streak of union elections, with no sign of slowing." NPR, April 14, 2022

106. Jodi Kantor and Karen Weisse, "The Morning: Amazon vs. the Union." New York Times, April 15, 2022.

107. Kantor and Weise, "Amazon Labor Union"

108. Lauren Kaori Gurley, "Amazon Cracks Down on Organizing After Historic Union Win." Vice, April 13, 2022.

109. Ibid.

110. Ken Klippenstein, "Leaked: New Amazon Worker Chat App Would Ban Words Like "Union," "Restrooms," "Pay Raise," and "Plantation." The Intercept (First Look Institute, April 4, 2022)

111. Hadero, Halleluya and Anne D'Innocenzio. "Amazon workers in NYC reject union in a reversal of fortune. Associated Press, 5 May 2022.

112. Hogan, Gwynne. "Two more union organizers fired from Amazon's Staten Island warehouse" Gothamist, May 9, 2022

113. Angus Loten and Adam Janofsky, "Sellers Need Amazon, but at What Cost?," The Wall Street Journal (Dow Jones & Company, January 14, 2015), https://www.wsj.com/articles/sellers-need-amazon-but-at-what-cost-1421278220.

114. Dana Mattioli, "Amazon Scooped Up Data From Its Own Sellers to Launch Competing Products," The Wall Street Journal (Dow Jones & Company, April 24, 2020), https://www.wsj.com/articles/amazon-scooped-up-data-from-its-own-sellers-to-launch-competing-products-11587650015.

115. Sam Schechner and Valentina Pop, "EU Starts Preliminary Probe into Amazon's Treatment of Merchants," The Wall Street Journal (Dow Jones & Company, September 19, 2018), https://www.wsj.com/articles/european-union-probing-amazon-s-treatment-of-merchants-using-its-platform-1537367673?mod=article_inline.

116. Rana Foroohar, Don't Be Evil: How Big Tech Betrayed Its Founding Principles--and All of Us (New York, NY: Currency, 2019), 181.

117. Ibid.

118. Devin Leonard, Neither Snow nor Rain: a History of the United States Postal Service (New York, NY: Grove Press, 2017), 251.

119. Ibid.

120. Christopher Shaw, First Class: The U.S. Postal Service, Democracy, and the Corporate Threat (San Francisco: City Lights, 2021).

121. Lina M. Khan, "Amazon's Antitrust Paradox," The Yale Law Journal, January 2017, https://www.yalelawjournal.org/note/amazons-antitrust-paradox.

122. Lauren Kaori Gurley, "'I Had Nothing to My Name': Amazon Delivery Companies Are Being Crushed by Debt," VICE, March 7, 2022

123. Ibid.

124. Ibid.

125. Ibid.

126. O'Donovan, "The Cost of Next-Day Delivery"

127. Ibid.

128. Ibid.

129. Ibid.

130. Ibid.

131. Ibid.

132. Ibid.

133. Ibid.

134. Lauren Kaori Gurley, "Amazon's AI Cameras Are Punishing Drivers for Mistakes They Didn't Make," VICE, September 20, 2021

135. Ibid.

136. Ibid.

137. O'Donovan, "The Cost of Next-Day Delivery"

138. Ibid.

139. Annie Palmer, "Amazon Flex Drivers Are Using Bots to Cheat Their Way to Getting More Work," CNBC (CNBC, February 10, 2020), https://www.cnbc.com/2020/02/09/amazon-flex-drivers-use-bots-to-get-more-work.html.

140. Ibid.

141. Ibid.

142. Rose Adams, "Big Business Games the Supply Chain," The American Prospect, February 9, 2022

143. Frontline Empire: The Rise and Reign of Jeff Bezos, PBS (Public Broadcasting Service, 2020), https://www.pbs.org/wgbh/frontline/film/amazon-empire/.

144. Foroohar, Don't Be Evil 238

145. Frontline Empire: The Rise and Reign of Jeff Bezos, PBS (Public Broadcasting Service, 2020), https://www.pbs.org/wgbh/frontline/film/amazon-empire/.

146. "Ring Inc.," Wikipedia (Wikimedia Foundation, May 8, 2020), https://en.wikipedia.org/wiki/Ring_Inc.

147. Susan Holmberg, "The Techlash Is the First Step to Restoring a Fair Us Economy," Financial Times, February 15, 2022

148. Audrey Conklin, "1 In 10 Police Departments Can Now Access Videos from Millions of Consumers' Ring Security Cameras," Fox Business, May 19, 2021

149. Jason Kelley Kelley and Matthew Guariglia, "Amazon Ring Must End Its Dangerous Partnerships With Police," Electronic Frontier Foundation, June 24, 2020, https://www.eff.org/deeplinks/2020/06/amazon-ring-must-end-its-dangerous-partnerships-police.

150. Matthew Guariglia, "Five Concerns about Amazon Ring's Deals with Police," Electronic Frontier Foundation, August 30, 2019, https://www.eff.org/deeplinks/2019/08/five-concerns-about-amazon-rings-deals-police.

151. Gita Jackson, "Dystopic Tiktok Trend Demands Amazon Workers Dance for Surveillance Cameras," VICE, February 3, 2022

152. Ibid.

153. Guariglia, "Five Concerns".

154. Abhishek Mishra, "Machine Learning in the AWS Cloud: Add Intelligence to Applications with Amazon SageMaker and Amazon Rekognition," Amazon (Sybex, a Wiley brand, 2019), https://aws.amazon.com/rekognition/.

155. Amrita Khalid, "Microsoft and Amazon Are at the Center of an ACLU Lawsuit on Facial Recognition," Quartz (Quartz, November 5, 2019), https://qz.com/1740570/aclu-lawsuit-targets-amazons-rekognition-and-microsofts-azure/.

156. Jacob Snow, "Amazon's Face Recognition Falsely Matched 28 Members of Congress With Mugshots," American Civil Liberties Union, June 28, 2019, https://www.aclu.org/blog/privacy-technology/surveillance-technologies/amazons-face-recognition-falsely-matched-28.

157. Ibid.

158. Drew Harwell, "Amazon Met with ICE Officials over Facial-Recognition System That Could Identify Immigrants," The Washington Post (WP Company, October 24, 2018), https://www.washingtonpost.com/technology/2018/10/23/amazon-met-with-ice-officials-over-facial-recognition-system-that-could-identify-immigrants/.

159. Kate Cox, "Leaked Pics from Amazon Ring Show Potential New Surveillance Features," Ars Technica, April 22, 2020, https://arstechnica.com/tech-policy/2020/04/ring-cameras-may-someday-scan-license-plates-and-faces-leak-shows/.

160. Lauren Goode and Louise Matsakis, "Amazon Doubles Down on Ring Partnerships With Law Enforcement," Wired (Conde Nast, January 7, 2020), https://www.wired.com/story/ces-2020-amazon-defends-ring-police-partnerships/.

161. Adam Smith, "Amazon Ring Working on Doorbells That Detect People by Their Skin and Smell," The Independent (Independent Digital News and Media, December 16, 2021)

162. Foroohar, Don't Be Evil 240

163. John Naughton, "More Power to IBM for Turning Its Back on Toxic Facial Recognition," The Guardian (Guardian News and Media, June 13, 2020), https://www.theguardian.com/commentisfree/2020/jun/13/silicon-valley-has-admitted-facial-recognition-technology-is-toxic-about-time.

164. Karen Weise and Natasha Singer, "Amazon Pauses Police Use of Its Facial Recognition Software," The New York Times (The New York Times, June 10, 2020), https://www.nytimes.com/2020/06/10/technology/amazon-facial-recognition-backlash.html.

165. Emily Birnbaum, "Amazon's Ring Has 29 New Police Agreements since the Killing of George Floyd," Protocol (Protocol, June 15, 2020), https://www.protocol.com/amazons-ring-police-partnerships.

166. Edward Ongweso, "UCLA Abandons Plans to Use Facial Recognition After Backlash," Vice, February 19, 2020, https://www.vice.com/en_us/article/z3by79/ucla-abandons-plans-to-use-facial-recognition-after-backlash.

167. Laura Hautala, "UCLA Cancels on-Campus Facial Recognition Program after Backlash," CNET (CNET, February 19, 2020), https://www.cnet.com/news/ucla-cancels-on-campus-facial-recognition-program-after-backlash/.

168. Kate Conger, "Amazon Workers Demand Jeff Bezos Cancel Face Recognition Contracts With Law Enforcement," Gizmodo (Gizmodo, June 22, 2018), https://gizmodo.com/amazon-workers-demand-jeff-bezos-cancel-face-recognitio-1827037509.

169. Paige Leskin, "Amazon's Public Policy Exec Got Booed in a Meeting with New York Council Members When He Evaded a Question about the Company's Business with Immigration Agencies," Business Insider (Business Insider, December 12, 2018), https://www.businessinsider.com/amazon-ice-government-provides-facial-recognition-tech-2018-12.

170. Brian Dumaine, Bezonomics: How Amazon Is Changing Our Lives and What the World's Best Companies Are Learning from It (New York, NY: Simon & Schuster, 2020), 110.

171. Ibid. 111

172. Foroohar, Don't Be Evil, 17

173. Jeb Su, "Why Amazon Alexa Is Always Listening To Your Conversations: Analysis," Forbes (Forbes Magazine, July 30, 2019), https://www.forbes.com/sites/jeanbaptiste/2019/05/16/why-amazon-alexa-is-always-listening-to-your-conversations-analysis/.

174. Mark Wilson, "Alexa's Creepy Laughter Is A Bigger Problem Than Amazon Admits," Fast Company (Fast Company, July 10, 2018), https://www.fastcompany.com/90163588/why-alexas-laughter-creeps-us-out.

175. "Alexa Tells 10-Year-Old Girl to Touch Live Plug with Penny," BBC News (BBC, December 28, 2021)

176. Mark Wilson, "Alexa's Creepy Laughter Is A Bigger Problem Than Amazon Admits," Bloomberg.com (Bloomberg, March 9, 2018), https://www.bloomberg.com/news/articles/2019-04-10/is-anyone-listening-to-you-on-alexa-a-global-team-reviews-audio.

177. Ibid.

178. Leo Kelion, "Amazon: How Bezos Built His Data Machine," BBC News (BBC, 2020), https://www.bbc.co.uk/news/extra/CLQYZENMBI/amazon-data.

179. Ibid.

180. Ibid.

181. Ibid.

182. Nick Statt, "Amazon Sent 1,700 Alexa Voice Recordings to the Wrong User Following Data Request," The Verge (The Verge, December 20, 2018), https://www.theverge.com/2018/12/20/18150531/amazon-alexa-voice-recordings-wrong-user-gdpr-privacy-ai.

183. Ibid.

184. Will Evans, "Inside Amazon's Failures to Protect Your Data: Internal Voyeurs, Bribery Scandals and Backdoor Schemes," Reveal, November 18, 2021

185. Ibid.

186. Ibid.

187. David Priest, "Buckle up: Alexa Is Asking the Questions Now," CNET (CNET, July 31, 2020), https://www.cnet.com/news/buckle-up-alexa-is-asking-the-questions-now/.

188. Ibid.

189. Ibid.

190. Alexandra Berzon, Shane Shifflett, and Justin Scheck, "Amazon Has Ceded Control of Its Site. The Result: Thousands of Banned, Unsafe or Mislabeled Products," The Wall Street Journal (Dow Jones & Company, August 23, 2019), https://www.wsj.com/articles/amazon-has-ceded-control-of-its-site-the-result-thousands-of-banned-unsafe-or-mislabeled-products-11566564990.

191. Ibid.

192. Ibid.

193. Ibid.

194. P.J. Bednarski, "USPS, Amazon, Google, PayPal Most Trusted Brands," MediaPost (MediaPost Communications, January 14, 2020), https://www.mediapost.com/publications/article/345638/usps-amazon-google-paypal-most-trusted-brands.html.

195. Louise Matsakis, "Amazon Quietly Removes Some Dubious Coronavirus Books," Wired (Conde Nast, March 11, 2020), https://www.wired.com/story/amazon-quietly-removes-coronavirus-books/.

196. Spencer Sunshine, "Amazon's Still Selling Lots of Nazi Books," The Daily Beast, January 25, 2022

197. Mattioli, "Amazon Scooped Up Data From Its Own Sellers to Launch Competing Products".

198. Ibid.

199. Aditya Kalra and Steve Stecklow, "Amazon Copied Products and Rigged Search Results, Documents Show," Reuters (Thomson Reuters, October 13, 2021)

200. Ibid.

201. Josh Dzieza, "Prime and Punishment," The Verge (The Verge, December 19, 2018), https://www.theverge.com/2018/12/19/18140799/amazon-marketplace-scams-seller-court-appeal-reinstatement.

202. Ibid.

203. Ibid.

204. Ibid.

205. Ibid.

206. Juozas Kaziukėnas, "Amazon Marketplace Is the Largest Online Retailer," Marketplace Pulse (Marketplace Pulse, December 3, 2018), https://www.marketplacepulse.com/articles/amazon-marketplace-is-the-largest-online-retailer.

207. Dzieza, "Prime and Punishment"

208. David Dayen, "Amazon's Attack on Women's Health," The American Prospect, November 19, 2021

209. Kaziukėnas, "Amazon Marketplace"

210. Stacy Mitchell, Ron Knox, and Zach Freed, "Report: Amazon's Monopoly Tollbooth," Institute for Local Self-Reliance, August 21, 2020

211. Ibid.

212. Mitchell, "Toll Road"

213. Ibid.

214. Cory Doctorow, "Amazon's $31b 'Ad Business' Isn't ," Pluralistic , February 27, 2022

215. Ibid.

216. "Everything on Amazon Is an Ad," Marketplace Pulse (Marketplace Pulse, February 25, 2021)

217. Ibid.
218. Krista Brown, "Rollups: The Gators Defining the Merchant Makeover," The American Prospect, February 10, 2022
219. Ibid.
220. Doctorow, "Ad Business".
221. Brown, "Rollups".
222. Ibid.
223. Ibid.
224. Doctorow, "Ad Business"
225. This quote is from a clipping I found in one of two boxes of Raven paraphernalia that original owner Pat Kehde donated to the Kansas Historical Society, much to the dismay of other original Raven owner Mary Lou Wright. Mary Lou reminds us frequently, when she comes to the store to buy books using rolls of quarters, that she didn't approve of Pat's donation. The reason I can't give you an exact date is because the article has been cut out, meaning the part of the masthead with the date is not visible. It's for an article about the tenth anniversary party, which would have happened in September 1997.
226. Again, the date has been cut off, but it's an article in advance of Borders's November 1997 opening in Lawrence.
227. Paris Marx, "Jeff Bezos Thanks Amazon Workers for Blue Origin Launch in Revealingly Tone-Deaf Moment," NBCNews.com (NBCUniversal News Group, July 21, 2021)
228. Rebecca Heilweil, "How Bad Is Space Tourism for the Environment? and Other Space Travel Questions, Answered.," Vox (Vox, July 25, 2021)
229. Alec MacGillis, Fulfillment: America in the Shadow of Amazon (New York: Picador, 2021)
230. Annie Palmer, "Amazon Wins Naming Rights to New Seattle Stadium and Will Call It the Climate Pledge Arena," CNBC (CNBC, June 25, 2020)
231. Ibid.
232. Brad Plumer, "Power Plants Are No Longer America's Biggest Climate Problem. Transportation Is.," Vox (Vox, June 13, 2016)
233. Miguel Jaller, "Online Shopping Is Terrible for the Environment. It Doesn't Have to Be.," Vox (Vox, December 21, 2017)
234. Ibid.
235. Ibid.
236. Emily West, Buy Now: How Amazon Branded Convenience and Normalized Monopoly (Cambridge, Massachusetts: The MIT Press, 2022), 75
237. Ibid. 75-76
238. Ibid. 75
239. Dorey Scheimer and Meghna Chakrabarti, "The Prime Effect: The Environmental Footprint behind the World's Largest Online Retailer," The Prime Effect: The Environmental Footprint Behind The World's Largest Online Retailer | On Point (WBUR, July 9, 2021)
240. MacGillis, Fulfillment 316.
241. West, Buy Now 79
242. Will Evans, "Private Report Shows How Amazon Drastically Undercounts Its Carbon Footprint," Reveal, February 25, 2022
243. Ibid.
244. West, Buy Now 79
245. Evans, "Private Report"
246. Ibid.
247. Ibid.
248. By April Glaser and Leticia Miranda, "Amazon Workers Demand End to Pollution Hitting People of Color Hardest," NBCNews.com (NBCUniversal News Group, May 25, 2021)
249. Amazon Employees for Climate Justice, "How Amazon's Emissions Are Hurting Communities of Color," Medium (Medium, June 24, 2020)
250. Kaveh Waddell and Maanvi Singh, "When Amazon Expands, These Communities Pay the Price," Consumer Reports, December 9, 2021
251. Ibid.
252. Ibid.
253. Ibid.
254. Hurwitz, "Warehouse"
255. Ibid.
256. Peter Beech, "What is Environmental Racism?" Global Policy Journal, August 4, 2020
257. MacGillis, Fulfillment, 12
258. Kate Conger, "Tech Workers Got Paid in Company Stock. They Used It to Agitate for Change.," The New York Times (The New York Times, December 16, 2018)
259. "An Airline Bailout Is Taking Shape (Coronavirus Briefings)," The New York Times (The New York Times, April 14, 2020)
260. Ibid.
261. Ibid.
262. Elizabeth Warren, et al. May 6, 2020 letter to Jeff Bezos. Senate.gov.
263. Tim Bray, "Bye, Amazon," ongoing by Tim Bray ·, May 4, 2020
264. Karen Weise, "Amazon Illegally Fired Activist Workers, Labor Board Finds," The New York Times (The New York Times, April 5, 2021)
265. Karen Weise, "Amazon Settles with Activist Workers Who Say They Were Illegally Fired.," The New York Times (The New York Times, September 29, 2021)
266. Kevin Killian, Selected Amazon Reviews Vol. 3 (New York: Essay Press, 2017)
267. Ibid.
268. Ibid.
269. Kate Durbin, "Art about Amazon Expresses Vulnerable Humanity in the Face of a Ubiquitous Behemoth," ARTnews.com (ARTnews.com, March 6, 2020)
270. Liat Berdugo and Emily Martinez, The Future of Work (Anxious to Make, 2016) 6
271. Angie Waller, Grifting 2
272. Angie Waller, Data Mining the Amazon (New York: Unknown Unknowns 2003)
273. Durbin, "Art"
274. Ibid.
275. Evan Minsker and Matthew Strauss, "The Black Madonna Released from Amazon's Music Festival after Tweeting Outrage," Pitchfork (Pitchfork, October 17, 2019)
276. Aaron Grech, "JPEGMAFIA Latest Artist to Drop out of Amazon's Intersect Festival Lineup ·," mxdwn Music, November 28, 2019
277. Allison Hussey, "Red Rocks Amphitheater discontinues Amazon Palm Scanning Tech," Pitchfork (Pitchfork March 10, 2022)
278. Elizabeth Weise, "Amazon HQ2 Timeline: The Winners Are New York City and Arlington, Virginia," USA Today (Gannett Satellite

Information Network, February 14, 2019), https://www.usatoday.com/story/tech/science/2018/09/12/timeline-amazons-search-hq-2-its-second-headquarters/1273275002/.

279. Matt Day, "Cities Crank up Publicity Stunts as Amazon's HQ2 Bid Deadline Arrives," The Seattle Times (The Seattle Times Company, October 20, 2017), https://www.seattletimes.com/business/amazon/cities-crank-up-publicity-stunts-as-amazons-hq2-bid-deadline-arrives/.

280. Louise Matsakis, "Why Amazon's HQ2 Search Backfired," Wired (Conde Nast, November 14, 2018), https://www.wired.com/story/amazon-hq2-search-backfired/.

281. Darla Mercado, "The Holiday Is over: Amazon Will Collect Sales Taxes Nationwide on April 1," CNBC (CNBC, March 24, 2017), https://www.cnbc.com/2017/03/24/the-holiday-is-over-amazon-will-collect-sales-taxes-nationwide-on-april-1.html.

282. Richard Rubin, "Does Amazon Really Pay No Taxes? Here's the Complicated Answer," The Wall Street Journal (Dow Jones & Company, June 14, 2019), https://www.wsj.com/articles/does-amazon-really-pay-no-taxes-heres-the-complicated-answer-11560504602.

283. "After a Decade—and More than $4 Billion—Watchdog Group Says: 'Time to Quit Subsidizing Amazon,'" Good Jobs First, March 1 2022

284. Hayley Peterson, "Amazon Gained a Huge Perk from Its HQ2 Contest That's Worth Far More than Any Tax Break," Business Insider (Business Insider, December 14, 2018), https://www.businessinsider.com/amazon-hq2-search-data-2018-11.

285. MacGillis, *Fulfillment* 32

286. Ibid. 33

287. Ibid. 33

288. Alex N. Press, "Amazon is creating company towns across the United States," Jacobin, July 24 2021

289. Ibid.

290. MacGillis, *Fulfillment* 32

291. Nathan Bomey, "Was Amazon's Headquarters Search 'a Giant Ruse'? NYC, D.C. Centers of Power Prevail," USA Today (Gannett Satellite Information Network, November 13, 2018), https://www.usatoday.com/story/money/2018/11/13/amazon-headquarters-hq-2-search-process-giant-ruse/1986577002/./

292. Reis Thebault Eli Rosenberg, "Amazon Had New York City in the Bag. Then Left-Wing Activists Got Fired up.," The Washington Post (WP Company, February 15, 2019), https://www.washingtonpost.com/nation/2019/02/14/how-amazons-big-plans-new-york-city-were-thwarted-by-citys-resurgent-left-wing/.

293. Kari Paul, "Alexandria Ocasio-Cortez on Amazon's New New York City Offices: I Told You So," The Guardian (Guardian News and Media, December 7, 2019), https://www.theguardian.com/technology/2019/dec/06/amazon-new-york-city-offices-lease.

294. Stacy Mitchell and OOlivia LaVecchia, "Report: Amazon's Next Frontier: Your City's

Purchasing," Institute for Local Self-Reliance, February 24, 2021

295. Ibid.

296. Ibid.

297. Daniel Lippman and Emily Birnbaum, "The Secret behind Amazon's Domination in Cloud Computing," POLITICO (POLITICO, June 4, 2021)

298. Sam Biddle, "Amazon Co-Owns Deportation Airline Implicated in Alleged Torture of Immigrants," The Intercept, February 17, 2022

299. Jake Alimahomed-Wilson and Charmaine Chua, "Amazon's Investments in Israel Reveal Complicity in Settlements and Military Operations," The Nation, June 22, 2021

300. Anonymous google and Amazon Workers, "We Are Google and Amazon Workers. We Condemn Project Nimbus," The Guardian (Guardian News and Media, October 12, 2021)

301. Aaron Gordon and Lauren Kaori Gurley, "Amazon Paid for a High School Course. Here's What It Teaches.," VICE, January 26, 2022

302. Sam Dangremond, "What Will Happen to Jeff Bezos' Massive Home in Washington, D.C.?," Town & Country (Town & Country, April 4, 2019), https://www.townandcountrymag.com/leisure/real-estate/news/a9234/jeff-bezos-house-washington-dc/.

303. Dayen, Monopolized

304. Ibid.

305. Robinson Meyer, "How to Fight Amazon (Before You Turn 29)," The Atlantic (Atlantic Media Company, June 12, 2018), https://www.theatlantic.com/magazine/archive/2018/07/lina-khan-antitrust/561743/.

306. Lina M. Khan, "Amazon's Antitrust Paradox," The Yale Law Journal - Home, January 2017, https://www.yalelawjournal.org/note/amazons-antitrust-paradox.

307. Ibid.

308. Sheelah Kolhatkar, "Lina Khan's Battle to Rein in Big Tech," The New Yorker, November 25, 2021

309. Ibid.

310. Ibid.

311. David Streitfeld, "As Amazon Rises, So Does the Opposition," The New York Times (The New York Times, April 18, 2020), https://www.nytimes.com/2020/04/18/technology/athena-mitchell-amazon.html.

312. Ibid.

313. Ibid.

314. Kolhatkar, "Khan's Battle".

315. Helene Fouquet and Matt Day, "Amazon Has a Europe Problem: Unions and Regulators Are Circling," Bloomberg.com (Bloomberg, April 30, 2020), https://www.bloomberg.com/news/articles/2020-04-30/amazon-has-a-europe-problem-unions-and-regulators-are-circling.

316. Valentina Pop and Sam Schechner, "WSJ News Exclusive | Amazon to Face Antitrust Charges From EU Over Treatment of Third-Party Sellers," The Wall Street Journal (Dow Jones & Company, June 11, 2020), https://www.wsj.com/articles/amazon-to-face-antitrust-charges-from-eu-over-treatment-of-third-party-sellers-11591871818?mod=searchresults.

317. Foo Yun Chee, "EXCLUSIVE Amazon seeking to settle EU antitrust investigations, sources say" Reuters (November 9, 2021)

318. Roth, Emma. The EU could start enforcing rules to regulate Big Tech in spring 2023. The Verge, May 8, 2022

319. Fouquet and Day, "Amazon Has a Europe Problem"

320. Ibid.

321. Ibid.

322. Porter Anderson, "Fixed Book Prices in Germany: Two New Studies Are Introduced in Berlin," Publishing Perspectives, November 8, 2019, https://publishingperspectives.com/2019/11/fixed-book-prices-in-germany-two-new-studies-borsenverein-released-berlin/.

323. News Wires, "France Moves to Shield Local Bookstores from Amazon with Law on Minimum Delivery Charge," France 24 (France 24, October 25, 2021)

324. Emma Jacobs, "France's Indie Bookstores Thrive in the Age of Amazon," Marketplace, April 29, 2019, https://www.marketplace.org/2016/01/28/frances-indie-bookstores-thrive-age-amazon/.

325. Lucy Koch, "Which Retailers Dominate Western Europe's Ecommerce Market?," eMarketer, January 29, 2019, https://www.emarketer.com/content/amazon-dominates-eu-5-ecommerce-market.

326. Mimi Montgomery, "Here Are the Floor Plans For Jeff Bezos's $23-Million DC Home," Washingtonian, August 1, 2018, https://www.washingtonian.com/2018/04/22/here-are-the-floor-plans-for-jeff-bezos-23-million-dc-home/.

327. Frontline Empire: The Rise and Reign of Jeff Bezos, PBS (Public Broadcasting Service, 2020), https://www.pbs.org/wgbh/frontline/film/amazon-empire/.

328. Dana Mattioli, "Amazon Scooped Up Data From Its Own Sellers to Launch Competing Products," The Wall Street Journal (Dow Jones & Company, April 24, 2020), https://www.wsj.com/articles/amazon-scooped-up-data-from-its-own-sellers-to-launch-competing-products-11587650015.

329. Dana Mattioli and Ryan Tracy, "Amazon CEO Jeff Bezos Called to Testify Before Congress," The Wall Street Journal (Dow Jones & Company, May 1, 2020), https://www.wsj.com/articles/amazon-ceo-jeff-bezos-called-to-testify-before-congress-11588343537.

330. Jess Del Fiacco and Stacy Mitchell, "Stacy Mitchell's Statement on Jeff Bezos Being Called to Testify Before Congress," Institute for Local Self-Reliance, May 1, 2020, https://ilsr.org/stacy-mitchell-statement-on-jeff-bezos-called-to-testify/.

331. Franklin Foer, "The Tech Giants Are Dangerous, and Congress Knows It," The Atlantic (Atlantic Media Company, July 29, 2020) https://www.theatlantic.com/ideas/archive/2020/07/tech-giants-are-dangerous-and-congress-knows-it/614740/.

332. Rebecca Klar, "House Panel Refers Amazon to DOJ for Potential Obstruction of Justice," The Hill (The Hill, March 9, 2022).

333. David Dayen, "The Triumphant Return of Congress," The American Prospect, July 30, 2020, https://prospect.org/power/triumphant-return-of-congress-big-tech-antitrust-hearing/.

334. Foer, "Tech Giants"

335. Jerrod Nadler and David Cicilline, et al., "Investigation of Competition in Digital Markets: Majority Staff Report and Recommendations, Subcommittee on Antitrust, Commercial, and Administrative Law of the Committee on the Judiciary." (United States, 2020), 7.

336. Ibid., 391

337. Shirin Ghaffary and Sara Morrison, "What You Need to Know about the House's Opening Bid to Rein in Big Tech," Vox (Vox, June 11, 2021)

338. Rebecca Klar, "House Advances Five Bills Targeting Big Tech after Overnight Slugfest," The Hill (The Hill, June 24, 2021)

339. Lauren Feiner, "Senate Committee Votes to Advance Major Tech Antitrust Bill," CNBC (CNBC, January 20, 2022)

340. Ibid.

341. Chris Gregory, Dr Regine Sonderland Saga and Professor Cathy Parker, "Booksellers as Placemakers The Contribution of Booksellers to the Vitality and Viability of High Streets" Institute of Place Management, February 2022

342. Ben Saunders, "Who's Using Amazon Web Services? [2020 Update]," Contino, February 20, 2020, https://www.contino.io/insights/whos-using-aws.

343. Sam Allard, "Excitement Over Cleveland's Brewery Explosion Has Given Way to Questions of a Brewery Bubble," Cleveland Scene (Cleveland Scene, April 28, 2020), https://www.clevescene.com/cleveland/excitement-over-clevelands-brewery-explosion-has-given-way-to-questions-of-a-brewery-bubble/Content?oid=5017228.

344. Olivia Solon, "As Tech Companies Get Richer, Is It 'Game over' for Startups?," The Guardian (Guardian News and Media, October 20, 2017), https://www.theguardian.com/technology/2017/oct/20/tech-startups-facebook-amazon-google-apple.

345. Rana Foroohar, Don't Be Evil: How Big Tech Betrayed Its Founding Principles--and All of Us (New York, NY: Currency, 2019), xvi

346. Megan Elliott, "How to Cancel Your Amazon Prime Membership," Showbiz Cheat Sheet, November 17, 2018, https://www.cheatsheet.com/money-career/how-to-cancel-your-amazon-prime-membership.html/.

347. Russel Brandom. "Using the Internet Without the Amazon Cloud." The Verge: July 28, 2018.

348. Franklin Foer, "Jeff Bezos's Master Plan," The Atlantic (Atlantic Media Company, November 8, 2019), https://www.theatlantic.com/magazine/archive/2019/11/what-jeff-bezos-wants/598363/.

ABOUT THE AUTHOR

Danny Caine is a co-owner of Raven Book Store in Lawrence, Kansas, the 2022 *Pubishers Weekly* Bookstore of the Year. He is the author of the poetry collections *Continental Breakfast, Picture Window, El Dorado Freddy's,* and *Flavortown*. He was has been featured in the *New Yorker* and named the 2019 Midwest Bookseller of the year. He is a passionate advocate, online and off, for independent, brick-and-mortar bookstores. DannyCaine.com.